The Candidates

The Candidates

Amateurs and Professionals in French Politics

ÉTIENNE OLLION

Translated from French by
KATHARINE THROSSELL

OXFORD
UNIVERSITY PRESS

Oxford University Press is a department of the University of Oxford. It furthers
the University's objective of excellence in research, scholarship, and education
by publishing worldwide. Oxford is a registered trade mark of Oxford University
Press in the UK and certain other countries.

Published in the United States of America by Oxford University Press
198 Madison Avenue, New York, NY 10016, United States of America.

© Oxford University Press 2024

All rights reserved. No part of this publication may be reproduced, stored in
a retrieval system, or transmitted, in any form or by any means, without the
prior permission in writing of Oxford University Press, or as expressly permitted
by law, by license, or under terms agreed with the appropriate reproduction
rights organization. Inquiries concerning reproduction outside the scope of the
above should be sent to the Rights Department, Oxford University Press, at the
address above.

You must not circulate this work in any other form
and you must impose this same condition on any acquirer.

Library of Congress Cataloging-in-Publication Data
Names: Ollion, Étienne, author.
Title: The candidates : amateurs and professionals in french politics / Étienne Ollion.
Other titles: Candidats. English
Description: First edition. | New York, NY : Oxford University Press, [2024] |
Includes bibliographical references and index.
Identifiers: LCCN 2023032526 | ISBN 9780197665954 (hardback) |
ISBN 9780197665961 (paperback) | ISBN 9780197665985 (epub) |
ISBN 9780197665978
Subjects: LCSH: France. Parlement (1946-). Assemblée
nationale—History—21st century. | Legislators—France—Social
conditions—21st century. | France—Politics and government—2017-
Classification: LCC JN2863 .O45 2024 | DDC 328.44/073—dc23/eng/20230809
LC record available at https://lccn.loc.gov/2023032526

DOI: 10.1093/oso/9780197665954.001.0001

Paperback printed by Marquis Book Printing, Canada
Hardback printed by Bridgeport National Bindery, Inc., United States of America

To Marie

CONTENTS

INTRODUCTION ... 1
   Militant Certainties and Scientific Questions ... 5
   A Sociologist in the House ... 9
   The Illusion of a Renewal ... 14
   Waiting Lines and the Making of *Homo Politicus* ... 17
   Outline of the Book ... 21

1. DOWN WITH CAREER POLITICIANS! ... 23
   The Cyclical Return of an Old Criticism ... 25
   Political Careers from a Historical Perspective ... 29
      Two Major Changes ... 30
      The Expansion of the Political Reserve Army ... 36
      2017, a Populist Moment for the French Elites? ... 39
   A Brutal Reconfiguration ... 43
      2017, an Atypical Campaign? ... 43
      Realignments ... 47

2. A PALACE WAR, NOT A REVOLUTION ... 52
   Changes in the House ... 54
      New Kids on the Floor ... 54
      An Original Selection Procedure ... 58
   Throw the Bums Out? ... 61
      Pathways to National Politics ... 62
      Operation Warp Speed ... 69
      The Moral Economy of the Waiting Line ... 74

3. UP-AND-COMERS ... 79
   Can Parliamentary Success Be Measured? ... 82
   Parliaments as Hierarchical, Differentiated Spaces ... 85
      Using Machine Learning to Represent Parliamentary Activity ... 86
      Unequal Life Chances ... 92
   The Passing of Time ... 96
      Knowledge and Acquaintances ... 96
      Waiting and Expectations ... 101

4. LIFE CHANGES ... 107
   A Dilated Time ... 109
   The Aristocratic Use of Time ... 113
   Becoming Public Property ... 116
   Striking Blows and Making Deals ... 121

5. THE PASSION FOR POLITICS   130
   Decreasing Returns   132
      Work More to Earn Less   132
      The Relegation of Parliament   137
      A Money Problem?   141
   Exploring the Political *Illusio*   143
      The Power to Do and the Right to Represent   144
      High-Intensity Life   147

CONCLUSION: IN THE WAITING LINE   153
   The Politics of Waiting Lines   154
   Waiting Lines Everywhere   156

Epilogue   161
Acknowledgments   167
Notes   169
References   175
Index   181

INTRODUCTION

It was a little after 1 pm on June 20, 2017, in the Palais Bourbon, the seat of the French National Assembly. A new legislative session was about to begin, and the new MPs, elected only days earlier, had arrived on the premises. On this first day, they could look forward to going through a long list of administrative formalities. They could be seen moving from one office to another, filling out forms, getting the key to their office, or retrieving their badge. They also collected their parliamentary insignia: the tricolor sash, an emblem that would adorn their vehicle for the next five years, as well as the *baromètre*, an elegant but discrete brooch that signals their status as a lawmaker. Despite the blistering heat outside, all were in formal attire, no doubt having been told in advance they would sit for official photos in the *hémicycle*, the iconic semi-circular chamber of the National Assembly, with its 577 dark red velvet seats.

Along the way, they filed past the crowd of journalists present for the occasion. These included the regulars—a dozen full-time correspondents who spend their weeks roaming around this former palace—together with those who cover question time, who generally attend only on Tuesdays and Wednesdays. But today was different, and the usual spectators were clearly outnumbered. Dozens of news reporters were on site, probably more than a hundred. The ambiance, too, was different, not the least in the Salle des Quatre-Colonnes, the official interface where journalists and politicians can meet. The whole place was abuzz with activity and bustling with people, some clearly not familiar with the locale. At one point, I even spotted entertainment reporters among those thronging in the vestibule; they gave the impression of being lost, as if they did not quite know where to look, or what to look at.

Arguably, this legislature was special. In the wake of Emmanuel Macron's triumph in the presidential election just a month before, a very unusual parliamentary cohort had been ushered in. Of these new MPs, 72% had never been elected to parliament before, where this figure is rarely over 40% in normal years. The landslide victory of Emmanuel Macron's party, En Marche! (EM)[1] also saw a record number of incumbents eliminated, some of them fixtures on the French political scene, while a number of new faces sparked surprise. But this renewal was not in itself enough to explain the flock of journalists or the unusual atmosphere. More than a simple alternation of political power, more than a massive changeover of personnel, the 15th legislature of the French lower house was marked by a record number of political novices, people with little to no experience in politics. And it was these individuals, who had become quite rare on the national political stage in recent decades, who occupied center stage.

For an observer in the halls of the Palais Bourbon, the new arrivals were easy to spot. Some appeared amused, others bewildered. They were often awestruck as they moved from one room to another. They spent time taking photos, alone or in small groups. They sometimes looked a bit awkward, too. As I waited in the *hémicycle*, the room where the plenary sessions are held, while MPs queued to have their official portrait taken, a few asked, tourist-style, if I could "take a picture" of them, which was immediately sent to family and friends. And while lingering in the Salle des Quatre-Colonnes, I found myself called on to act as an impromptu guide. One MP asked me the way to the men's room, another asked directions to his own office. Yet another first-time MP turned to me to ask if she was allowed to answer questions from a journalist. The overall ambiance was more that of a school excursion than a return from parliamentary recess.

The contrast with the previous legislature, which I had also studied, was striking. It was the consequence of a rather atypical election, especially by the standards of French politics. Nothing had gone according to plan during the two campaigns that had culminated that spring; the presidential election in May immediately followed (as has been the case since 2002) by legislative elections the following month. The incumbent socialist president, François Hollande, hampered by the internal dissidence in his party that had marred the end of his mandate, by opposition to his policies, and by his own massive unpopularity, had announced late in the day that he would not seek a second term. But more surprises were still to come. Imported from the United States during the 2000s as a badge of "modernity," the use of party primaries to select candidates for the major parties produced unexpected results. On both the right and the left, the process led to the nomination of the contenders with the most radical programs, in the form of Benoît Hamon—from the left wing of the Socialist Party (PS)—and François Fillon, on the hard right of Les Républicains (LR).

Another surprise was the emergence of Hollande's former minister of economics, Emmanuel Macron, as an official candidate in the race, after months of discrete campaigning. Not even 39 years old, Macron had begun his career in politics only a few years earlier, after working as an investment banker. Unlike all of his predecessors, he had never held elected office at any level. His campaign launch in November 2016 thus elicited real interest, thanks in part to its novelty, together with a great deal of skepticism concerning his prospects. So much so that when Macron won the presidency in May, and a sizable parliamentary majority in June, commentators and political scientists alike were left to marvel at how the stars had aligned so perfectly in his favor.

The greatest surprise of the campaign, however, came from elsewhere. Macron's platform, reiterated week after week by his team, was truly unusual. Typically, candidates run on subjects outside the political field itself, such as taxes, immigration, health, or the environment. This was not the case for the leader of EM, who for months insisted on one theme: the need for new blood to revive French politics. He claimed the political sphere was obstructed by the presence of too many career politicians, accused of putting their own strategies and chances for re-election over the well-being of the country.

During one of his first public meetings, even before he formally announced his candidacy, Macron made democratic renewal his central message. In an appearance in Strasbourg on October 4, 2016, the former cabinet member—he had resigned from Hollande's government a few weeks earlier—laid out his vision of the state of French politics. It was bleak. Democracy had been "confiscated" by special interests for too long. In his eyes, union and business representatives did not reflect society; the voting system worked to prevent the expression of certain ideas. Political parties no longer attracted "talent." But Macron's most serious accusation was directed at politicians. They were accused of making a mere "occupation" out of the noble calling of politics, of pursuing narrow "self-interest" over the common good. For Macron, the political class with its antiquated habits was the main culprit for the crisis of confidence that had beset the country.

Democratic inertia was not a new theme for Macron at this point. Back in May 2016, when his nascent movement had barely started fundraising, an email later revealed by the press spelled out this same charge in no uncertain terms. Sent to several dozen potential donors while Macron was still a cabinet member, its message was clear; resources had to be found to support a future candidate who would "crack open a system in which politics has become a matter of seasoned professionals," to breath fresh air in a "nauseating milieu."[2] For Macron and his supporters, politics had become "professionalized," an occupation in its own right. It was the exclusive domain of a handful of politicians, a "cast" that had to be removed from power.

This line of argument would be hammered home repeatedly over the year that led the young candidate to victory and the Élysée Palace, the residence of the French president. In many ways it was remarkable that it should be an up-and-coming technocrat and ex-minister who took up this fight. Hitherto, this charge against professional politicians had chiefly been mobilized by less centrist parties and figures, both in France and other countries. All over Europe, this theme had bought resounding success to the parties that used it, from Italy's Movimiento 5 Stelle (Five Stars Movement), created by the actor Beppe Grillo in 2013, to Spain's Podemos (We Can), a party created in 2014 on a platform of political renewal. Even Donald Trump's vow to "drain the swamp" in Washington was part of the same repertoire. Also a political outsider, the multimillionaire businessman focused his campaign on railing against current officeholders. His electoral platform, baptized the "Contract with the American Voter," began with a demand for term limits for all members of Congress.[3] Although unconstitutional, the measure was often presented as an expression of his desire to shake up the political ecosystem by bringing in not only "new people," but also "a different type of people."

The resonance of Macron's repeated call to usher in new faces must be understood in this light. For at least two decades, criticism of the monopoly over political power exercised by a small number of elected representatives has grown louder and louder. In France as elsewhere, the figure of the political "professional"—a polysemic term that suggests long experience of operating inside the political field—served as a convenient, if not indispensable, trope. Never the most popular figure, the "career politician" became a kind of bogeyman that had to be dispensed with, while its antithesis, the political novice, emerged as a perfect alternative, a solution to most of our ills.

How did this abrupt reversal happen? Looking at the French case in-depth, while drawing on other polities for comparative purposes, this book investigates the intensity of these calls for political renewal. Vituperations against politicians aside, other signs have likewise indicated a desire for a more inclusive democracy. The increasing appeal of direct democracy (promoting referendums, popular initiatives), the proliferation of "citizen" ballots in various elections, or the return of techniques long considered unrealistic, such as sortition (random selection) of representatives, were all signs of an interest in involving laypeople in public life. As we shall see, it was not only the appetite for political change that conferred on the 2010s its markedly "antiprofessional" hue. This period also saw the culmination of a shift in political careers that stretches back nearly half a century, in France and in Europe more widely.

At the same time, this book raises another, more complex question, with implications that extend well beyond the French and European context. It investigates whether and to what degree the past trajectory of political leaders has an impact on their practice of politics, and on the functioning of democracy overall. The answer has important implications for the claim that a renewal of the political personnel can have the transformative effect implicitly assumed by those who clamor for renewal, that a change in casting might transform the entire show. Demands to replace "career politicians" with representatives from more varied career backgrounds are premised on the belief that the arrival of novices will change politics, for the better. The replacement of long-time representatives by laypeople is assumed to introduce new ways of thinking and acting to a hermetic, self-involved sphere. But is there any evidence of this assumption? This ramifications clearly go beyond the case of EM, or indeed France. Ultimately, it comes down to questioning what the "professionalization" of politics does to politics in practice, or even more broadly: what does political experience do to the practice of politics?

Militant Certainties and Scientific Questions

The question of what determines how elective representatives behave has been analyzed since the origin of parliamentary systems. This is partly because it reflects the foundation of representative democracy. Indeed, if belonging to a social group or following a particular political trajectory influences political practice and behavior, if what (and who) representatives are or what they have been determines the way they represent citizens, then the whole mechanism of delegation is thrown into question.

Back before the French Revolution, the American founding fathers questioned the ability of those who were elected to provide "substantive" representation regardless of their backgrounds. Even among federalists the question was thorny; James Madison wrote in *The Federalist Papers* (no. 52) that it was preferable that those in government had "an intimate sympathy" with those they represented, where Hamilton considered this a risk and was less opposed to the British hereditary system.

Since then, the question has been the subject of hundreds of scientific studies, perhaps even thousands. This body of research seeks to understand the impact of a particular social quality or situation (gender, social background, regional or ethnic origin, or disability, for example) on the way politics is conducted. Even before the introduction of the distinction between descriptive representation and substantive representation by Pitkin (1967), there were regular debates on the idea that the presence in politics of people belonging to a particular group could influence the way in which the interests of that group were represented.[4] And, as both parliaments and governments almost never represent the wider society (Best & Cotta, 2000; Evans & Tilley, 2017), this question remains relevant today. In fact, it is all the more salient because the schism between voters and their political elites—which can be clearly seen in the mistrust toward politicians visible in many societies—only makes this issue more pressing.

Surprisingly, the role of political experience on political practice has been less studied. Assertions by militants that professionalized representatives are less invested in the general interest, or are only motivated by their own re-election, or even that they conduct politics differently, by no means meet with scientific consensus.

Of course, nothing would be more misguided than to assert that the topic was never an object of study. Back in the early 1960s, political scientist Donald Matthews differentiated between American senators based on their parliamentary behavior (1960). After he examined their path to the Senate, Matthews saw a strong connection between political practice, institutional structure, and past trajectory. But he also considered this research exploratory. However stimulating, his argument hinged on only a handful of typical cases that were not systematically analyzed. A decade later, his colleague H. Douglas Price also took up this question, this time focusing on the 19th century American Congress. In this context, where representatives all had another primary profession, politics was practiced quite differently. Resignations were frequent, which led to high turnover rates and more frequent shifting of coalitions (Price, 1975). The results were telling, but the book fell short of studying the effect of the experience on individuals. In addition to being dated, these results were aggregated, making it difficult to identify a causality between individual careers and political practice. Any individual effect could, at best, only be deduced from collective variations.

This is also the question posed in David Canon's book on amateurs in the US Congress (1990), where the author tests the link between candidates' political background and their behavior in Congress. The book is rich: it builds on a few classics (Wilson, 1962) and it summarizes a vast amount of existing literature on adjacent topics. It also leverages empirical materials, both on careers and on practice, that were at the disposal of the author at that time. His response is a prudent yes, given that the data is hard to collect, and according to him not always conclusive, at least at the individual level. Since then, few studies have successfully identified a professionalization effect on practices. This might come as a surprise given the extent of criticism leveled against professional politicians, but one would be hard-pressed to find definitive evidence, one way or the other. In what is probably the most precise and recent work on this question, political scientist Peter Allen extensively reviewed the literature on the topic (2014), and he came to the same conclusion. To him, large aspects of this topic were still waiting for a definitive answer.

When it comes to knowing whether a parliament of novices would do politics differently, the scientific evidence tends to respond with a tentative, nuanced yes that requires further research. But ironically enough, when it comes to knowing whether novices would change politics for the best, as Macron kept promising during the 2017 campaign, the existing scientific evidence tends to point the other way. In the 1990s, the introduction of a maximum number of mandates in state-level local legislatures made room for less experienced representatives to move into politics. This provided US political scientists with an interesting field experiment to analyze the potential ability of political novices to return power to laypeople. The results were mixed at best. Various studies conducted using this change in legislature converged to attest to a loss of influence for legislative bodies. The arrival of representatives who were unfamiliar with the political game shifted the balance of power, sometime drastically, toward the executive and the administration (Kousser, 2005). Other scientific studies, like those initiated after a gender parity reform forced political parties to select more women as their candidates for different elected position, confirm these results. Novice women thrown into this unfamiliar milieu had trouble finding their place among their more established peers and were consequently relegated to second-order tasks (Achin, 2016).

Arguably, despite the fact that they are both relevant, these types of studies are not looking at the same object. While the latter type often focuses on particular individuals (or just a few) in order to make sense of their complete experience, the former looks mostly at the aggregate level, comparing legislatures. This limits the conclusions that can be drawn for all individuals at a given moment, which points to a larger problem, one that explains why definitive results on the role of experience are hard to reach. Overall, any investigation into this area is plagued by two measurement difficulties.

Firstly, characterizing a politician's background is harder than one might think. Beyond the data issues that I will soon return to, the question of what a career politician (and by opposition, a novice) actually is, raises many questions. Is a person a "professional politician" if they have spent decades in politics? If they have spent only a few years, but all of their adult life, in the political sphere? Or should we stick with the oft-evoked Weberian definition of the professional as the one who lives "off" politics at a given moment? But in this latter case, all politicians are professionals as soon as they get elected, and that is probably something few would disagree with, otherwise politics would be reserved for plutocrats.

Clearly, terms such as. "career politician," "professional politicians," and a few others that are often treated as synonymous, conceal a variety of trajectories behind one signifier. The growing criticism against "political professionalization" in Europe and the emergence of the term in the public sphere certainly has not helped, as it has gone hand-in-hand with an even wider diversification of its meanings. This observation was recently made by researchers in an overview of the literature on the British case. They noted that in the wake of increased academic attention, the concept has been "stretched to cover an ever-wider variety of cases, while the spotlight has shifted from one definitional dimension to another" (Allen et al., 2020, p. 210).

The second reason the role of the practical experience of politics has not received the scientific attention it deserves is that this would require connecting two types of research that each tend to stop on either side of the doors to parliament. As Peter Allen has correctly noted (2014), most analyses focus on preparliamentary careers, as they try to account for what makes some people more likely to be elected. Using different methods, they document what it takes to stand and later to win an election, describing the typical pathways to power.[5] The other group of analysis focuses on practices, on what MPs end up doing once they are in parliament.[6] Of course, many studies in one area evoke the other aspect, but few do it in a symmetrical way, dedicating as much energy to one aspect as to the other. There are sound empirical reasons for this. Both types of analysis require a heavy investment. Preparliamentary careers can be traced, but at the cost of painstaking—some would even say punishing—data work. Parliamentary practice can also be analyzed, but even with the new abundance of digital data, the question of what MPs spend their time doing remains hard to answer decisively. Not all the available information is relevant, and all relevant variables are not readily available; moreover, even if one were to access all the information required, there is no obvious statistical technique that can treat such multidimensional data. That is why most quantitative studies focus on only one parliamentary practice (votes, legislative work, media participation, etc.).

Finding ways to measure these two aspects, and consequently analyzing what political experience does to the practice of politics, is precisely what I set out to do in this book. Looking in detail at the careers of French MPs before they entered parliament, but also investigating the practice of every one of them on a wide variety of activities after their election, I was hopeful that I could provide fresh answers to this nagging question. The election of a brand-new legislature in 2017, with hundreds of newcomers and dozens of complete political novices working alongside seasoned politicians who had been saved from the political tsunami initiated by Macron, provided me with this unique opportunity.

A Sociologist in the House

As Emma Crewe wrote in her study on Westminster, parliaments have everything an anthropologist desires: "Conflict sits with co-operation. Friends and foes argue, soothe and perform curious rituals, and hierarchies shift around" (2015, p. 1). So there is nothing surprising about the fact that several social sciences studies have been done on these spaces known for their order and rituals. Some 20 years ago, Marc Abélès demonstrated the benefit of this kind of monographic approach in the case of the French Parliament (Abeles, 2000), and many of his observations remain relevant today. The same holds true for social scientists more generally. Because most of the action happens in a confined space, parliaments are a fantastic theater for politics, a stage where an observer can capture and analyze the fabric of everyday politics probably better than anywhere else.

This explains why I did not hesitate for long when I was offered the opportunity to study this institution, back in 2015. I had heard from a colleague that a senior official was looking to invite social scientists to conduct research on the parliament. Naturally, we both had conditions; I wanted to be given a reasonably free access to most spaces, the right to interview MPs, but also officials, staffers, and lower-ranking employees. She wanted me to be discreet, and not disturb the orderly organization of the space. My presence, she worried, could raise some eyebrows. Although over 2,000 people work in this building every day, and although many groups come for tours, she was anxious that having a sociologist freely wandering the corridors of the Palais Bourbon might appear a bit eccentric. But she was also curious enough, and we came to an agreement. I would have the same access rights as a parliamentary journalist, but I could also access data and archives, and she would help organize for me to observe in different departments, at my request. In the end, she provided valuable help in navigating the intricacies of this old palace where tradition still holds an important place. These rights evolved over the course of the study, sometimes more generous, sometimes less, but I never felt I was constrained in my study.

But the main reason for my decision to study the French National Assembly has to do with the role that the lower house plays in political life in France. Although its role has been somewhat reduced in the semipresidential system of the Fifth Republic, it remains a key stage in political careers. Unlike in parliamentary regimes, it is not necessary to be an MP to be a cabinet member. Macron himself went directly up the political ladder—he was for a time the economy and finance minister—without having ever been elected. This is, however, not the standard pathway, as nearly two-thirds of future government ministers are first recruited to the lower house (Behr & Michon, 2015). The remaining third, who are appointed from civil society, often turn to the National Assembly for a position once their time in government is over. A quasi-obligatory stage along the path to accessing roles of greater responsibility, the lower house is also, in France, the first echelon in national politics. It is the one place where older, experienced representatives who have been involved in politics for decades rub shoulders with ambitious young delegates, for whom this is an initial foothold. This was especially true in 2017, with the arrival en masse of hundreds of new MPs whose time and past positions in politics ranged from the highly experienced, with over 40 years in national politics, to complete novices who had had no prior political engagement whatsoever. From the point of view of the study I wished to conduct, the National Assembly was nothing short of what the North American sociologist Robert Merton called "a strategic research site," a prime location through which to access a larger reality—the political field.

To take this further, I wanted to supplement this ethnographic approach with statistics. My intuition was that the questions raised above, which were also voiced in the public sphere, about the role of experience in politics, could finally be answered if I were to find new, fine-grained individual data on how MPs carry out their work. This relied on the promise of the booming field of computational social sciences. This multidisciplinary endeavor rests on two pillars: one is to make the most of the abundant data to ask old or new but always scientifically relevant questions; and the second is to leverage the power of computers to provide better responses to classic investigations. In my case, I resorted to machine learning algorithms to investigate parliamentary activity in a more refined way. And in this endeavor, ethnography would help locate and interpret the relevant data, while the algorithms would help me cast a new light on it.

This was the plan, and it seemed to work at the beginning. From 2015 to 2017, I often returned to the Parliament. Most of the time I was alone, but sometimes students I was supervising tagged along. Over these two years, I was able to conduct dozens of interviews with MPs, staffers, journalists, and other people present on the premises. My students also conducted interviews, thus helping me multiply the points of view on this protean institution. Meanwhile, I began collecting biographical data. The idea was to gather original good-quality data to measure what had changed in the careers of these elected representatives. Along with two colleagues—Julien Boelaert and Sébastien Michon—I set out to entirely reconstruct the professional and political trajectories for all the MPs over five legislatures since the 1970s.

In my naiveté, I thought this would be an easy task. Biographies are often available online, on Wikipedia, and even on the official website of the National Assembly. But I quickly realized that they are largely misleading. Upon arriving in the House, MPs are free to choose what they declare in their biographies, and they often "polish" them to suit the image of themselves they wish to promote. Unsurprisingly, very few MPs wrote "career politician," "politician," or "former parliamentary assistant" in the space reserved for their occupation. Whether real or perceived, the risk of being immediately disqualified for such a description is too great.

This problem was endemic, as I quickly found out. One socialist frontbencher mentioned on his biography that he was a "senior private sector manager" even though his last professional position outside of politics dated to a two-year temporary position back in the early 1990s. After the socialists' massive defeat in the legislative elections in 1993, he had not managed to find a fallback position due to a lack of openings, so he spent a few years working in the private sector. This professional experience was short-lived, as he was elected a few years later and then remained within politics. But thirty years later, it was this short stint that he put in the "occupation" section of his official profile. Other examples are just as emblematic. Former prime minister Manuel Valls listed his profession as "communication advisor," a post he held—after entering politics—when he was a young aide in the cabinet of Michel Rocard, another prime minister. As for François Fillon, the right-wing champion in the 2017 presidential election, on the Assembly page, he indicated that he had "no occupation,"[7] even though he had held one of the prime parliamentary staffer positions in the Assembly since 1978, before embarking on a long and very successful career as an elected official.

The truth, as I painfully discovered, is that MPs are very strategic about the identities they put forward in these biographies. As a result, I could not trust the online biographies and other open data repositories that have become more numerous in recent years. To get around these issues, I had to do it the old way, the hard way. Through a collective effort, the biographies of more than 2,400 MPs were therefore pieced together by hand from various sources. The information was retrieved from the archives of the National Assembly, from local media, obituaries, and from Wikipedia pages and LinkedIn profiles for the most recent candidates. We double checked them wherever possible and looked for inconsistencies. In practice, we collected all the available information on careers in and outside of politics for each MP and for each year of their adult life after age 20 (before that, data was patchy). Some points remained uncertain at the end, but for the most part they were resolved. This effort to create a consistent prosopography that reflects the careers of political actors on such a large scale is, to my knowledge, unprecedented. It provides us a detailed overview of national-level political careers over the course of the last half-century in France.

It was supplemented by individual-level data on how MPs practice politics. One again, my approach was inductive. I first studied MPs in their milieu, tried to uncover the many ways one can invest oneself in parliamentary activity. Only then did I look for data that would help me operationalize these criteria. This method runs counter to a practice that has become standard in (bad) science, one that tends to look for a data set—possibly one that is available online—and then declares it fit to respond to the question. To study parliament, I could have resorted to one of these databases that are compiled by institutions or civil society organizations. They display a series of disconnected and not always relevant metrics, such as the number of times a given MP spoke in a committee, or the number of amendments she submitted. Against this quantophrenic approach, I spent days collecting data I deemed relevant for the problem at hand, searching beyond the information immediately available.

The research process took longer than I initially intended. My initial plan was to write an empirical book on the rise of professionalism in French politics. I did so with two colleagues (Boelaert et al., 2017). But shortly after it was released in April 2017, the book was already out of date. The electoral season, with its share of surprises and the massive replacement it had produced, made some of our conclusions about the tendency toward political professionalization defunct. In other words, the renewal ushered in by Macron abruptly turned my sociological opus into a history book. The arrival of nearly one hundred political novices at the Palais Bourbon completely changed the political landscape. The seemingly unstoppable rise of professionalism had come to a (temporary) end. Yet this new situation provided an unprecedented opportunity to test many of the hypotheses expressed in the various studies on professionalization, including those explored at the end of the book I had just published. Even before the results of the second round were in, I negotiated my return to the halls of Parliament. This time, I was granted a generous security clearance that enabled me to observe the new legislature in operation over more than a year. So, I again took up my interviews, observation, and data collection. Around 30 interviews were conducted with MPs and various other figures who gravitate around the small world of the Palais Bourbon. An additional 50 interviews were conducted by my students as part of a research seminar I cotaught for four years. Countless more informal conversations also happened over the course of my fieldwork. These were not recorded, but were duly noted in my notebooks—and they often yielded more interesting results with respondents, who often confused me for a journalist.

This book thus presents the results of this extended investigation. In addition to the aforementioned quantitative data, it combines archival material, research notes from extensive observation sessions, and excerpts from interviews. It shows individuals who act, argue, insult each other, or trade in low blows. It presents them through their lived experience of everyday politics, in an attempt to uncover who they are. It does not, however, provide any names or elements that would enable the identification of these representatives. Most of the participants have been anonymized and there are two main reasons for this. The first is essential to the research pact I established with them. I promised my interviewees anonymity and could not revoke that once the fieldwork was finished. It would be impossible to betray such trust. But there is a second reason, which is equally important in my eyes. Several of the figures in the book are well known, at least to a French audience, and a handful would be familiar to an international audience. Others will become so in years to come. Quoting them by name would probably provide additional information to some readers, but it would also personalize the analysis, when I want to emphasize the fact that these are individuals acting within a broader structure that guides their action.

The argument is that the individuals in this book act under a host of constraints—their past careers as well as their current positions. Thus, in addition to adding a potential bias to the narrative, depending on the information and opinions of the reader, naming interviewees would run counter to my general argument about the role of experience in politics. Following the existing conventions in sociology, individuals are therefore referred to by pseudonyms in order to preserve their anonymity, and the information necessary to understand their situation (like their education or social background) is provided with this initial presentation. This choice is thus not just pragmatic and driven by the needs to conduct this study, it is also theoretical. It is based on my conviction, acquired as I was doing this research, that we should refuse to treat politicians any differently from other individuals that populate social scientific books. On the contrary, elected representatives would benefit from being described as ordinary men and women who, for a time, have pursued a specific career path. To study today's *homo politicus*, we must explore these people's history, their interests and passions, their values and their hopes, their labor and their suffering, as we would with any other sociological subject.

The Illusion of a Renewal

This research provides insights into the contemporary political world. The first result of this investigation is that the main promise made by the Macron campaign, namely that the massive influx of novice politicians would drastically modify the way politics is done, was not kept. For the most part, the 2017 novices did not successfully forge a place for themselves in the French political sphere. Despite their repeated efforts, only a handful of them managed to carry some weight during the legislature—a result that dovetails with the existing works on amateurs. The book then probes the reasons for that previous status quo. It expounds the causes that made these rookie MPs helpless, despite their undeniable will to make a difference and even sometimes the will of their party. Not only did they lack practical skills and knowledge, but they also had to adapt to a world in which the rules were already laid down but were largely unfamiliar to them. They also lacked the connections and necessary social capital that make politicians efficient. All of this, in turn, contributed to a dearth of the kind of self-assurance their established colleagues had in spades, and thus reinforced their inability to make their presence felt.

Despite an unprecedented renewal, re-elected MPs, as well as some newcomers with more political experience, snapped up the main positions of power. In particular, former staffers and parliamentary assistants monopolized top jobs in parliaments, exactly as they used to do before. Worse still, for those who supported the renewal proclaimed by EM during the campaign, the laymen who were elected following Macron's victory helped him shift the balance of power further away from the legislative branch and toward the executive. Encouraged to not challenge the party to which they owed everything, their presence meant that ministers, former cabinet members, and MPs well-versed in politics as it used to be, were free to operate in the most traditional way possible.

This conclusion should come as no surprise. There was a certain naiveté in the belief that a simple change in casting could deeply alter the functioning of the political sphere. This is not limited to *En Marche!* alone, or even to the French case. It forces us to critically examine certain responses that have gained popularity in recent years due to the crisis of political trust. Every election in recent memory has seen the emergence of independent candidates running without party backing, who share the belief that politics needs "new leaders" who will be able to bring radical transformation. They claim political amateurs will make better public leaders, that they will represent wider society more appropriately, and that once in power, they will do politics differently. What the French experience shows is that this belief is, at least in part, misguided. The change they aspire to will not happen merely by bringing in a few dozen, or even hundreds of individuals from different backgrounds. It will take much more to achieve the profound transformation they call for—and that is deeply needed.

Let me be clear. My goal here is not to flatly reject all these initiatives, and still less to discredit their demands. It is plausible that changing political figures, or at least some of them, may be necessary to achieve the shift that is desired. These initiatives also raise the essential question of the identity of representatives, their past, and their ways of doing politics, an aspect that is all too often concealed, especially in a country like France with its deeply entrenched universalism. Instead, my goal is to move the conversation forward, by looking at what prevented these novices participating fully, despite quite favorable conditions given that they arrived en masse. Using the French case, this book sets out to identify the origins of political inertia and to understand the logics that led to it. Based on a full-scale evaluation of this quasi-natural experiment—rather than on an abstract or extraordinary situation—it looks at why the introduction of novices into an existing institution will likely fail to produce the expected results.

This, in my view, should lead us to change the terms of the debate. Rather than asking ourselves whether a change in the political casting influences politics, we should explore under which conditions such a change could happen. The example of the French status quo can teach us much about the logics at work in this. Such inertia is largely the result of the fact that despite the massive turnover (for memory, there were 72% of newly elected MPs), the amateurs were encouraged to join a world in which the rules of the game had not changed, a world in which politicians with more experience knew the ropes and could impose their will. Responsibility for this, though, does not lie solely with more experienced MPs. The reason these new arrivals did not succeed is that they were not regarded as legitimate politicians by other actors—journalists, public officials, but also other citizens. Because they did not fit the commonly accepted idea of what a politician is, or does, novices were excluded from the political game, or they excluded themselves after having been publicly disqualified. To better understand the failure of this experiment, we need to get a better grasp of contemporary politics, to describe the milieu the novices were projected into. We need to follow them from their constituency to the parliament, from their house to their offices. Analyzing the experience of these new parliamentarians leads us to explore, and better understand, this highly specific activity that is professional politics.

Waiting Lines and the Making of *Homo Politicus*

Besides these empirical results, the book makes a broader, more theoretical contribution. It contends that to understand who political leaders are and explain why these novices failed, we may need to change the way we see careers in politics. As mentioned above, the 2017 campaign was centered on the idea of an increasing "professionalization of politics." The term was widely used by Macron's campaign team, but it had a broader appeal. Over recent decades, the term and its correlate noun (professional, or career politicians) had gained prominence in the public sphere. In fact, both terms were routinely used by journalists, candidates, and citizens. They also became an important subject in the social sciences, judging by the numerous books and articles published on the topic.[8]

This framing has its virtues. It was, for instance, instrumental in describing some fundamental changes that happened in the organization of politics in previous decades, as well as some that occurred more than a century ago. But analyzing contemporary politics with terms such as "political professionals," "career politicians," or "political professionalization" increasingly runs the risk of obscuring the analysis. The main reason is that these terms lump together people with different, sometimes hardly comparable, trajectories and attitudes toward politics. It is possible to be a national political actor, like an MP, and still share very little in the way of experience with one's colleagues. Local representatives who spent decades in power at the municipal or departmental level before they reached a national position late in their lives often have little in common with those who are parachuted into a constituency after a brief stint in a ministerial cabinet straight after graduating from Sciences Po—the school of the political elite in France. The dichotomy conceals highly divergent pathways into politics. Similarly, to describe the process that happened mainly in terms of "professionalization" may not adequately describe what has been happening in recent decades. If professionalism simply refers to someone who lives off politics, according to Weber's oft-evoked definition of professional politicians, then all French MPs have been professionals since 1852, when the parliamentary allowance was permanently reintroduced.

These difficulties are explored in the following chapters, along with other criticisms on the overreliance on the "professionalization" rhetoric to describe recent changes in political careers. For the moment, let us be content with saying that Max Weber's canonical distinction between those who live "for" and those who live "off" politics, or the distinction between "career" and "novices," does not do justice to the numerous questions raised by the recruitment of political representatives.

To analyze the transformations of the political field in recent decades, this book invites us to conceptualize political careers as a "waiting line," an ordered succession of positions where politicians must bide their time before accessing important roles. In this line, politicians learn the tricks of the trade, they create contacts that will later be useful, and they learn to appreciate politics.[9] The queue prepares them for their arrival in a position of power, it helps them adjust to the milieu they aspire to be part of. What is more, far from being the democratic device it could be, where everyone waits equally for their turn, these queues are also rife with inequalities—some wait for a long time, while others take the fast track.

As we shall see, this change in perspective is insightful. It shows that the central tendency in the French political sphere in recent decades has not been "professionalization," an inexorable increase in the number of political professionals unexpectedly interrupted by the 2017 election, but rather the development of an orderly queue for access to national-level elected positions. It explains the increased conformity of MPs, whether in terms of social background or of practices. It also explains the outcry that happened in 2017 when, in the wake of Macron, dozens of neophytes successfully managed to access positions of power.

The numbers are telling. From the 1970s to the mid-2010s, politicians spent an increasing amount of time waiting for their turn to access national mandates. In 1978, a French MP typically consecrated 12 years to politics before accessing parliament. This figure rose to a whopping 18 years in 2012, increasing the time spent in various political positions by 50%. It was this queue, which had been constantly increasing over the last four decades, that the 2017 novices "jumped," and with them other candidates who avoided part of it. The former did not even have the waiting period, they were immediately thrust onto the center of the national political stage, and the latter, who had some prior political experience, took the opportunity to save themselves a few years of patient progression. Both groups took advantage of the disruption created by Macron's new party, and by joining its ranks, they bypassed the traditional order of succession.

This book concretely demonstrates the relevance of an analysis of the contemporary political field in terms of this waiting line. It traces the beginning of this phenomena back to the mid-1970s in France, but also in other

European countries, and explains why this ordered progression has become a principle that structures access to national political positions in various countries. Then, through a comparison between elected representatives from the 2012 legislature and others from the 2017 legislature, it analyzes the ambivalent effects of these waiting lines on representatives, on the political field, and ultimately, on democracy. Trading the binary opposition between "professionals" and "novices" with the concept of the waiting line means we can restrict the idea of the professional politician to those who "live off" politics. This might seem like a sheer semantic dispute, but this shift in focus reveals other important aspects of political careers.

This change in perspective helps us draw insight from works that have explored the relationship between time, duration, and their impact on individuals. Literature is filled with situations where the experience of time passing is essential to the narrative. Vladimir and Estragon, the main characters in Beckett's *Waiting for Godot* are often quoted in descriptions of the powerlessness felt by those who wait. So is Joseph K. the antihero in Kafka's *The Trial*, whose attitude to the world is radically altered by his endless, aimless wait. Just as well-known and perhaps more directly linked to this question is *The Tartar Steppes* by Dino Buzzati. In this story, the soldier Giovanni Drago is sent to a garrison in an isolated fort where he can do nothing but wait for an enemy that legends suggest lies on the other side of the border, on a mountainous plateau. Over the course of the novel, the reader sees his view of the world progressively narrow as the years pass. His curiosity, his desire for change, but also his professional and family hopes are constantly scaled down to the point where the young ambitious soldier, who initially wanted to leave the camp quickly, ultimately ends up anxious at the idea of leaving the place where all his habits were forged. His wait for an invisible enemy has become the focus of all his practices, and has taken a toll on his desires.

However, this book draws above all on social scientific research, in which an abundant literature has analyzed the relationships between waiting, social status, and practice. These studies are mentioned throughout the book. What sets this research apart, however, is that it seeks to identify what is specific about the waiting line, what this framework does to the practice and to the representation of the individuals it entraps. In one pioneering study, Barry Schwartz laid the foundation for sociological research on this form of social organization (Schwartz, 1974), showing that queues are systems that reflect power relations within a society. Those who waited were most often those with the least resources. Through a range of examples, primarily Soviet shops and American airports (his two favorite illustrations), Schwartz showed that the poor waited more than anyone else. Even with time, social dynamics are refracted in daily situations. Javier Auyero later demonstrated this in a trailblazing study of the role of waiting in the disciplining of welfare recipients in Argentina (Auyero, 2012). While confirming the main results of Schwartz, he explored other dimensions of waiting, looking particularly at the way individuals reacted differently to it. Taking up the typical distinction between the duration (the subjective estimate of time passing) and time, he identified certain social determinants in the acceptance of the waiting period.

For political leaders, as in many other situations, the waiting line is not so much a concrete situation—a more or less well-ordered physical alignment of people—as it is a concept designed to reveal an otherwise invisible reality. This is the meaning that has been emphasized in other studies, such as that by Barbara Reskin and Patricia Roos, who used it to understand how women progress less quickly than men within companies (Roos & Reskin, 1990). Looking at how large US corporations deal with women, they revealed that some individuals manage to "cut in" to the line. Although they do not take the physical form of the long lines snaking outside shopfronts like in the Soviet bloc, which also received attention from sociologists,[10] the invisible queues they described nevertheless have an organizational pattern that some manage to avoid. The authors demonstrate the role of gender in the differential progression, as they stress the role of recruiters in selecting those to be promoted—once again according to gender principles. The lack of materiality, and thus of a clearly established and visible order, makes it easier for some individuals to progress faster than others.

These studies, as well as many others, are mobilized and sometimes discussed in the following chapters. The goal is to demonstrate the relevance of analyzing contemporary politics through the prism of the waiting line, and also to make this metaphorical concept more systematic. The book shows what this form of social organization does to individuals, to their ways of seeing and doing, and to the allocation of rare goods. More specifically, I argue that these waiting lines have three clear effects that can sometimes be observed in studies on waiting, but which must be considered together. Waiting lines are spaces where individuals are *socialized*, where they are *selected*. They are also places where groups are *individualized*.

As we will see, the concept is useful in reflecting on the major transformations that have been occurring in the political field. Waiting gives individuals time to learn, to be trained in the sometimes-complex functioning of parliament, and in the rules of the political game. We can see this in the difficulties encountered by novice MPs in the first months. Because they did not have time in the waiting line, they discovered at their expense that it takes a lot of practical knowledge to perform in politics. When the line *forms*, it also *conforms*. Socialization, but also peer selection, accounts better than anything else for the increasing homogeneity in both the profiles and actions often observed. The existence of a waiting line might provide fresh explanations for what has often been condemned since the 1980s as the "*pensée unique*," a common view held beyond party lines about what ought to be done. The chain of interdependence in which representatives—from the local level to the highest national levels—find themselves, produces conformity and restricts the space of possibilities.

Similarly, the uncertain waiting period that characterizes the candidates' situation has led to a selection process, which itself is a powerful driving force in the oft-attested social homogenization of the political class, whether in France or elsewhere. From the selection of successors by party leaders, and the self-selection that leads to elites distancing themselves from unstable and low-income activities, the concentration of upper-middle-class individuals among representatives can be explained by this recruitment process that is as subtle as it is effective.

Finally, waiting lines tend to individualize groups. They are certainly not anarchical spaces, devoid of any form of organization. Quite the contrary, ethnographies of queues have demonstrated how they are complex social objects heavily regulated by norms, including solidarity. But their ordered, hierarchical, and precarious structure does not transform them into instances prone to produce a common interest. They differentiate more than they empower, they antagonize more than they unify. This was perfectly illustrated when ambitious young politicians from both the left and the right broke ranks to join Emmanuel Macron in his victorious campaign, thus turning their backs on their bosses and mentors to seize this opportunity to significantly speed up their career.

Outline of the Book

This book takes us deep into politics, both past and present, while illustrating the merits of the concept of the waiting line. Chapter 1 starts in the midst of the action, with a presentation of the French political situation in 2017. It analyzes the renewed success of the criticism against career politicians in light of the long-term transformations that had occurred in political careers, both in France and abroad. Chapter 2 looks back at the rupture introduced by the 2017 election. Was it a people's revolt, as the new president's supporters liked to say, or was the *grand soir* of French politics just a palace revolution? Here again, historical perspectives and statistical data provide useful elements to address this question, while at the same time responding to the pressing question of whether French politics has become more "professionalized"? Chapter 3 addresses the central question of the role of experience in politics. Using original quantitative data and a little-used yet promising machine-learning method, it proposes a representation of a hierarchical and differentiated parliamentary space. These elements show how novices were relegated to unimportant positions, and the preservation of classical hierarchies between types of elected officials, which are then supported by more qualitative analyses. Chapter 4 dissects the experience of the novices after their abrupt emergence onto the national political stage. Like bodies immersed in a milieu they were not familiar with, they serve as analyzers in action within this highly codified space. Their stories collected in the early years of this legislature are rich with information about the structures and daily texture of politics. They also show how the past trajectory in the waiting line determines the experience that people have of politics. Finally, Chapter 5 asks, if political activity is so hard and so demanding, why—and who—does it attract? If it is not for the money, nor for the power—these two usual suspects are easily ruled out—then what? It then lays out a sociological explanation for what is often treated, in a pop-psychological fashion, as an addiction to power.

1
DOWN WITH CAREER POLITICIANS!

To anyone familiar with the French political scene, the 2017 election season felt atypical. Normally, during these moments of intense attention on politics, the main issues revolve around broad issues. Security, taxation, immigration, or more recently the environment, are more likely to capture the public's attention than the careers of political representatives. But not in 2017. That year the attention was focused on the biography of the political personnel, and the term "*les professionnels de la politique*" (professional politicians) became a ubiquitous insult in public debate. But neither in France nor abroad was this attention to the political elite fully unprecedented. Rather, it marked the latest revival of an insult that is as old as the compensation of politicians for their work.

The criticism of professional politicians had been widely revived over the previous decade. An apparently trivial example provides a good illustration of this. In blog post from September 2014, Michèle Delaunay, a former Socialist MP, lamented the arrival of a new generation into politics. According to her, those moving into national politics in the 2010s shared one trait: the vast majority of them had had no professional experience outside this milieu. Although she did not use the term "professional" or "career politicians," as such, her target was clear. "They graduate from Sciences Po [the school of the political elite], take an administrative exam, or not, they look around.... Then they get a position as a staffer or a local government job. The luckiest, or cleverest of them end up as a top aide to a cabinet member. In this ever so slightly limited world, they catch the bug."[1] Describing the stages in a well-oiled career, Delaunay, a former oncologist, observed at the end of her career that her youngest colleagues had less and less experience outside politics. The image she used is telling. She wrote that "they go into the tunnel early and never come out." According to her, the consequences are immense. Once they set out on this path, these ambitious young people "lose touch with reality and the sense of the common good." As they get older, they behave as if they are "beyond even the most basic rules."

This blog post was widely discussed in the political sphere because it echoed an experience that had been shared by many. Even beyond the inner circles of power, the idea that careers had changed had become commonplace. Since the early 2010s, the terms "professionals" or "professionalization" have become increasingly frequent when talking about politics.[2] These figures appeared at the heart of various intrigues, even in works of fiction. In many of the political-themed television series that have been produced in recent years, a common plot features political old guards rubbing shoulders with young ambitious graduates from the schools of power, already hungry for their political careers. Professionalization is sometimes even the primary theme.

In the Danish series *Borgen* (The Fortress) a young woman who was not meant to be in line for the position of prime minister is thrust into this role due to a last-minute political reshuffle. The series opens with a televised debate taking place a few days before the national election. The main character, a low-key figure on the Danish political scene, launches into an impassioned speech. Without notes and against the recommendations of her advisers, she rails on national TV against . . . career politicians. Against all polls, and thanks to this speech, her party ends up winning the election, making her the next prime minister.[3] The series follows her as she learns the norms and rules of this milieu, dodging low blows and navigating communication strategies. The advantages of political professionalization, but also its dangers for democracy, are two themes that run through the whole show.

During his entire campaign, Emmanuel Macron rode this antiprofessional wave. He hammered home this line of argument repeatedly over the year that led him to the Élysée Palace. Some observers may have found it surprising that the campaign was so strongly focused on this subject. Since the end of World War II at least, this antiprofessional rhetoric had mostly been mobilized by marginal political parties and figures. In the postwar period, French shopkeeper-cum-populist politician Pierre Poujade, founder of the *poujadist* movement in the 1950s, coined the slogan "sortir les sortants" ("kick out the incumbents") which would have a long legacy. One of the most famous to mobilize this rhetoric for decades was a former *poujadist* who would soon become the leader of his own far-right party, Jean-Marie Le Pen.

But it was highly thus unusual for someone with a background like Macron's, or parties in the same ideological line as En Marche!, to mobilize such a rhetoric. In 2017, the party was clearly running on a centrist platform, alternating between center-left and center-right propositions. Macron himself, the party leader, had followed the most typical path to French politics.[4] He was a graduate of Sciences Po and an alumnus of the elite school of government (ENA, or École nationale d'administration). He was also a former business banker who had become the main aide to the French president back in 2012. A few weeks before launching his bid for the presidency, he was still minister for the economy and finance. In other words, the future president of the French Republic did not have the typical attributes of the antisystem leaders who ordinarily rely on this rhetoric. In fact, despite having all the characteristics of the very elites shunned by those who express the antiprofessional discourse, he became its strongest promoter in the 2017 season. Apparently, this was not an impediment. Macron, arguably, was a bit different. Unlike his main rivals, the young candidate had not spent decades in politics, but just a few years. And despite having held top-level political offices, he had never previously been elected, nor even officially run for election. His relative inexperience, associated with being a relative outsider to political system, could be brandished aloft like a flag, in a context of intense denunciation of political professionals.

This chapter tries to account for this apparent puzzle. It shows that this act of political transubstantiation owes much to the structural transformations at play within the French political system over the last decades. During those years, the paths to access national politics had significantly changed. In particular, candidates for national-level elected positions had to spend a longer amount of time in politics before they were able to move into national positions. This was true in all the political parties, whether left or right, in government or not. This is what made the antiprofessional argument so effective in 2017. Without these significant, but often overlooked changes, chances are that Macron's critique would have fallen on deaf ears, and that his adventurous run for president would have been followed by a quick retreat.

The Cyclical Return of an Old Criticism

"Professional politicians" have a bad rep. This is as true today as it was when the term first appeared in the French language, around the late 1880s. Back then, newspapers were already discussing "professional politicians," and not in a good way. They described them as "self-interested, ambitious" (*Le Patriote*, April 1, 1899), cunning ("long experienced in the trade, and master of all its tricks," *La Revue*, 1900, p. 39), but also "dull" (*Le Petit Parisien*,

January 2, 1917) and "boastful" ("speaking publicly with the same ease as a professional politician," *Le Matin*, February 7, 1934, p. 2). They were also described as being different from their fellow citizens ("thus the voice of Mr. Doumergue affirmed the increased antinomy between the [...] professional and the man on the street," *Notre temps*, May 16, 1934, p. 3). Any number of examples could be given from among the hundreds of quotations from the press of the period, but one would be hard pressed to find more than a handful that would cast a positive light on this figure.

A precise study of the notion as it appeared in public and scientific debates in France was conducted two decades ago by political scientist Dominique Dammame. His conclusion is unequivocal: the term has had a negative connotation since it first emerged. Political professionals, he wrote, perform an "unenviable trade" (Damamme, 1999, pp. 37–68); they consistently act as a foil. The French term "*politicien*," a direct import from the English language, was adopted at that time to criticize those who regarded politics as a trade. A journalist first used it in the early 1900s, as he made a parallel between the French officeholders and the emerging figures involved in organizing political campaigns in the United States. Unlike in English, where it can be neutral, to call someone a "*politicien*" was no compliment. As the human incarnation of the "political machine" that mobilized the electorate in different constituencies to serve a political boss, these "*politiciens*" were more frequently praised for their dubious electoral prowess than for their defense of the common good. Over the years, the term "political professionals" came to be preferred in French public discourse, but the idea, and the negative symbolic charge, remained the same. Both today and in the past, they have been accused of pursuing victory for their political faction at any cost, as well as serving their own interests.

It is no coincidence that the epithet "professional," applied to politicians, appeared in the late 19th century, just when the practice of giving monetary allowances to elected representatives was becoming common practice. In national parliaments, later in other elected bodies, it became standard to offer representatives compensation for the time they invested in their role. All over Europe, this was a period of profound change in the way the political world was organized, and the fundamental cause for the emergence of what would be called professional politicians (Best & Cotta, 2000). It was in fact this very phenomenon, the shift from politics being mostly an unpaid activity to one resulting in financial remuneration that Max Weber was referring to when he proposed a definition of the professional politician. When he wrote his lecture "Politics as a Vocation" (Weber, [1919], 1946), the world he described was changing. This was, of course, the case in Europe, which was emerging from four years of unprecedented war and entering a new era of economic, moral, and intellectual reconstruction. But it was also more indirectly true for the political world over the previous half century. In the previous decades, the Western societies he mentions had undergone a vast movement of democratization. This movement was still incomplete, not the least because in nearly all of these countries women and other groups were excluded from suffrage, but elections had become widespread as a way of choosing political representatives. And politicians who had no personal resources could by then envision running as candidates, since compensations had progressively been introduced.

As Weber explains, compensation was not the norm until the mid-19th century at least. Until then, a national or a local representative had to be "economically 'dispensable' [abkömmlich], that is, his income must not depend upon the fact that he constantly and personally places his ability and thinking entirely, or at least by far predominantly at the service of economic acquisition" (Weber, [1919] 1946, 10). This lack of compensation for representatives had obvious effects on political recruitment. No workers, but also no members of the then nascent middle classes, could aspire to such an unstable and unpaid activity. Weber noted that this exclusion was not limited to the lower spheres of society. "The modern entrepreneur" could not be involved either because of the time constraints of their business. Recruitment was therefore "plutocratic," based on personal fortune and availability.[5]

Yet this system was challenged by the regime changes that would affect Europe over the course of the 19th century. As new representatives arrived and new social groups claimed their share of political power, the question of how they would be indemnified for their time became more pressing. In France, the parliamentary allowance has a chaotic history. It was established for representatives immediately after the Revolution, then abolished between 1814 and 1815, re-established under the Second Republic (1848), then again revoked at the beginning of the Empire, and then finally granted for good in 1852 (Borchert and Zeiss, 2003). The chronology differed in other European democracies, as did the amount paid to politicians, but the process was basically the same: a move toward stable, decent, and indisputable pay for full-time representatives.

It was in this context that Weber made his now-classic distinction between "living for" and "living off" politics. He was referring to those who used to lived "for" politics under the old system, and those, more common in the new world, who lived "for" politics, but also "off" it. It is important to note that this distinction is above all analytic and that it had no negative connotation: living off politics, receiving a compensation, was the fate of contemporary representatives, but also party officials, and American political "bosses," who were awarded public-sector jobs after a successful campaign. Weber was not judging the skills, qualities, or motivations of these people, but rather their ways of being in politics. His distinction above all pointed to a change in the rules of the political game at the turn of the 19th century.

In France, historian Éric Phélippeau has studied this transition period. He showed how the figure of the "modern politician," one that closely resemble our contemporary political leaders, was invented in these years (Phelippeau, 2002). Indeed, these evolutions meant the upheaval of the social organization of politics, and an increased competition for elected roles. This went hand-in-hand with the creation of specific institutions, political parties, and trade unions in the first place that would allow others to "professionalize," once again in the Weberian sense of allowing some of their members to "live off politics."

The introduction of a compensation for political work was not without criticism, even if it came almost exclusively from the right at the time. In an article on the first elected workers of the Paris Council in the 1880s, Michel Offerlé recounts the criticisms they faced (Offerlé, 1984). They were attacked on the grounds of incompetence but also for their "heavy and clumsy" physique, the criticism of transgressive bodies acting as a synecdoche for ways of acting and thinking, which were assumed to be equally unusual. But these criticisms were above all focused on venality because the candidates were accused of running purely to obtain an allowance. In 1882 the monarchist newspaper *Le Soleil* published the following diatribe against the remuneration of MPs: "The day when [elected positions] are demanded merely as one would demand a position as a rural guard, they will fall into depravity and be sought only by false workers, ignoramuses and sluggards, keepers of taverns and cabaret bars." The journalist went on to deplore the fact that the "representatives in the house and in the Senate have been made into a salaried condition, instead of allowing them to preserve their true nature as a political mandate."

In later years, as democratic regimes developed, the idea of remuneration gained footing and the criticism was no longer so marked politically. However, the term "professional politician" itself remained pejorative, often overlooking the fact that the "professionalization" of politics was also a condition of its democratization. The intensity of this criticism fluctuated, however. In the following decades, for example, it was not professionalization that was the greatest concern; corruption, venality, and self-interest become more central issues in public debates. The "bureaucratization" of representatives returned periodically to the fore, whether in the 1930s to refer to the remuneration of MPs by the state and fears of parliament's lack of autonomy, or in the 1980s when, with the election of a Socialist government for the first time in more than 20 years, the political right raised concerns about the massive arrival of public servants in parliament, who replaced the liberal professions that had been previously well represented.

It was only after the 2000s and particularly in the decade that followed, that the question of professionalization returned to the media agenda, slowly but surely gaining in intensity. This phenomenon was not limited to France. In England, the emergence of a group described as "career politicians" was identified as early as the 1980s, and it has been subject to many comments since then (King, 1981). Even in a country like Sweden, with a reputation for easy-to-access political positions (Hagevi, 2003), these criticisms started to emerge in recent years. A specific term even began appearing in public debates, "broilers." Literally referring to battery chickens, this English word was used in Sweden to describe and denounce representatives who had never had any professional activities outside politics. Raised within political parties before being thrust onto the national political stage at an early age, they were accused, like many of their European colleagues, of only ever having lived "off" politics.[6] To be sure, the accusations were not exactly the same as those of the previous century. The idea that MPs should be compensated was less central—although pay remained the key object of discussions. But the disconnect between wider society and individuals who have "never worked" outside of politics, along with their alleged self-serving behavior remained a central theme, as was the idea that politicians were acting in their own interest, or in the interests of their re-election.[7]

Political Careers from a Historical Perspective

Why has this long latent criticism of career politicians become more explicit and more frequent in recent years? And why did the ritual demand for a change in leaders by opposition parties turn into a request for the wholesale replacement of politicians by people who had little, or even no, political experience? To understand how such a shift could happen, it is important to recognize that political careers have changed drastically in recent decades, both in France and elsewhere. Just as a profound change took place in the way representatives were elected in the 1900s, another transformation of the same magnitude began occurring in the 1970s, although silently. The paths toward politics were changing again, which led to outcries about this rise in "professional politicians." As early as 1990s, in England, the parliamentary journalist Peter Riddell had already noted that "the career politician has become, if not the dominant, then at least the typical politician" (Riddell, 1995, p. 186). The same was true across Europe. While noting differences between countries, the authors of a comprehensive collective work published in the early 21st century documented the return of this issue across Europe (Borchert & Zeiss, 2003). With variations in scope and in timing, virtually all chapters in the massive volume pointed toward a rise in this "political professionalization."

Two Major Changes

The extensive research on the career of French politicians sheds light on these transformations. In an attempt to better understand who becomes a national politician, and how, I collected information on the personal trajectories—both political and biographical—of MPs under five different legislatures starting in the late 1970s. These cohorts were analyzed comprehensively, which meant compiling a full professional biography for all individuals who were elected to parliament during this term, year after year. I selected the legislatures carefully, alternating between right-majority parliaments and left-majority parliaments, while having the necessary historical distance to be able to observe long-term trends. Ultimately, this amounted to the reconstruction of more than 2,400 complete individual careers. As we shall see, the results are telling.

In the French political science literature, several indicators are often deployed to support the idea of a "professionalization of politics." One of them measures the number of MPs who have held a position as a staffer or political aide: as members of a ministerial cabinet, in the municipal team of a major city, or as a parliamentary assistant in the national or European parliaments. These are the individuals directly described as having "enter[ed] the tunnel" at a young age, in the words of Michèle Delaunay, the former minister quoted earlier.

In this respect there is a very clear evolution. From the 6th legislature (1978–1981) to the 14th legislature (2012–2017), the percentage of MPs who held one of these positions before being elected more than doubled, rising from over 14% to more than 32%. Growth was clear and consistent, 23% in 1997, 29% in 2007, and nearly 33% in 2012. This situation, it must be noted, was not specific to a particular party. In 2012, 36% of the Socialist representatives elected had followed this career path, only slightly more than their counterparts on the right (32%). Among the centrist parties, the proportions were roughly the same (38%) (Table 1.1).

The shift is clear, and it is not specific to parties in government. Of course, to be able to offer political employee positions, a party has to have cabinet members, or be present in parliament or local government. But other positions are accessible, whether as party officials, on regional councils, or among MEP staffers. In both regional councils and the European parliament, proportional representation opens up space for parties that are often otherwise excluded by the majoritarian voting system. The prime example of this comes from the far-right party Rassemblement National (RN). Its leader, Marine Le Pen, who inherited both her father's name and his party, was never an aide. She was, however, employed by the party only a few years after graduating from law school (1992), first as a legal advisor (1994), and then as an official when she became director of the legal team in 1998. Then she began her own career first as a regional representative (1998), and then as an MEP (2004). Her then partner, Louis Aliot, had been hired as cabinet director for Jean-Marie Le Pen, the president of what was then the Front

Table 1.1 Percentage of MPs who previously held a position as a political aide (in %, rounded)

	1978	1997	2007	2012
Right (RPR-DL then UMP-LR)	22	22	28	32
Left (PS, PRG)	6	24	34	36
Center (UDF, NC, UDI)	20	31	27	38
Others	3	4	18	21
Total	14	24	30	33

In 2012, 32% of the right-wing MPs had, at some point in their career, worked as a political aider (staffer, parliamentary aide or assistant, party employee).

National (FN), while also performing other paid functions. Beyond these individual cases, in 2014, five MEPs out of the FN's 20 had previously held political roles behind the scenes, and a few others had performed duties paid for by the party.

This evolution did not go unnoticed among party members. One long-term party executive expressed his concern about the massive influx of these aides in the party hierarchy:

> Relegating the rank and file to supporting roles, kicking out all the real party faithful and replacing them with young graduates [...] when you're twenty-three and already elected and you think you can be an MP next year, you remain loyal to whoever gave you that you that nomination. If that doesn't prepare someone to support the system, with the tools of the system ....[8]

This transformation is particularly salient in the context of internal party struggles. It nourished old militants' fear of a different type of "great replacement," in which old militants would be supplanted by a cast of young officials, accused of having seized power within the organization. Clearly a *cursus honorum* had developed, and as we will see below, obtaining one of these positions often meant more rapid ascension to power and more frequent appointments to ministerial roles.

But the most significant change in French politics between the 1970s and 2010s was not so much this rise in the number of former aides in national political positions, but something that received much less attention despite being far more widespread. This second deep-seated transformation is the vast increase in the amount of time spent in politics before gaining access to a national-level mandate. In 40 years, a spectacular lengthening of this path toward parliament had taken place. Between 1978 and 2012, time spent in politics before accessing a role in parliament, whether in an elected position or as an aide or an official, had increased by half, from 12 to over 18 years. Even more significant was the increase over this period for first-time representatives, doubling from 5.7 years to 11.6 years. In other words, a first-time MP in 2012 had spent twice as long—nearly 12 years on average—in politics than their 1970s counterpart before arriving in parliament.

These figures are even more telling when analyzed not in terms of total time spent in politics, but as a percentage of adult life (after age 20). In this case, the proportion goes from 44% in 1978 to 61.4% between 1978 and 2012. In other words, MPs elected in 2012 had spent nearly two-thirds of their adult life paid to work in politics. These figures do not take into account the potential years spent as militants in a party or youth organization, which is common for many. At the other extreme, the number of people who had no political experience before arriving in parliament has declined dramatically. In the 1970s it was around 10%, but has since dropped to insignificant figures.

Interviews conducted with MPs from the 14th legislature (2012–2017) are exemplary of these extended political trajectories. One socialist MP talked about his lengthy experience before he was elected in 2012:

> My last job was as cabinet director for a territorial authority. Before that I was a technical advisor to the president of the Ile-de-France [greater Paris area] region. Before that I was a staffer with the Socialist group in the Ile-de-France region. And before that staffer in a cabinet in a territorial authority.[9]

Another one, interviewed in 2005 by my colleague Sébastien Michon, perfectly illustrates this typical trajectory, but this time spent investing at the local level:

> By the time I was 30, I had already spent 15 years of my life as an apparatchik [laughs] between the MJS and the PS. After my master's program, I did my military service [in 1999]. When I finished, I joined the cabinet, working for the minister [the MP/mayor of the town he came from] as a low-level assistant. For me it was an extraordinary experience. It's true that being in a ministerial cabinet when you're 24 years old is an incredible opportunity for observation. [. . .] I was working with the assistant responsible for the local and regional committee. Then I went to the Regional Council with the Socialist and Green groups for over a year. Then I was a parliamentary assistant for six months. After the legislative elections [in 2002] I left to work with B. [mayor of a large town nearby]. I worked for all the MPs of the region [laughs]. While I was there, I was responsible for political questions, security, local issues. I stayed a bit more than two years. Then I came back here to work with R. [elected senator in 2004]. And now I want to become an MP myself . . . eventually, there's no point rushing things.[10]

In the years that followed, he would work as a parliamentary assistant in the constituency, before being elected deputy mayor in his hometown, as well as municipal councilor, and departmental councilor. In 2017 he had hoped to run for the legislative elections, but he was not endorsed by the party.

To be sure, these drawn-out career ladders to political power were not fully new. In fact, they had even been typical for a while . . . in the French Communist Party (PCF). Careful to preserve its image as the party of the working class, the PCF put in place a system of internal promotion which allowed a (patient) worker to successively become a local union rep, then a regional rep, then a party candidate, and eventually for a select few, an MP. Up until the 1970s, there were a few of these figures present in the parliament. One of the most well-known was the presidential candidate André Lajoinie, who had dropped out of school to help his parents on the family farm before becoming a party activist (1946), official (1954), and then party secretary, first locally and then in Paris (in 1957, then 1963). He would eventually become an MP for the first time in 1978. Any number of other examples could be given here of people who have climbed the party ladder in this way (Pudal, 1989).

In the early 2010s, however, the situation was quite different. The electoral demise of the Communist Party meant that this internal ladder was no longer available. But in the meantime, the model had spread to other parties. From right-wing parties to the Green Party, from the far-left to the far-right, the paths into politics had changed by the time Macron entered the race in late 2016. Figure 1.1 shows the time individuals spend in politics, as a percentage of their adult life, and clearly reflects this phenomena, on both sides of the political spectrum. For example, back in 1978, left-wing MPs spent 41% of their life in paid political positions, but by comparison, in 2007 their counterparts spent 68% of their lives in such positions. Although this figure somewhat decreased in 2012, this was mostly due to a change in the ruling party that year. The same dynamic can be seen both in the center and on the right; in fact, it can even be seen in nongovernment parties. In the last 40 years, the political field has closed in on itself, forcing the candidates, and even potential candidates, into a long probationary period in the form of time spent waiting in other paid political roles. Up until 2017, the barriers to politics had become higher: it was then almost impossible to gain access without having had previous long-term involvement in politics, to the point where no one could even consider it.

In the next chapter, I will analyze the different implications of this waiting period, imposed on those wanting to engage in politics. But it is important to note that this time the candidates must spend waiting adds another criterion

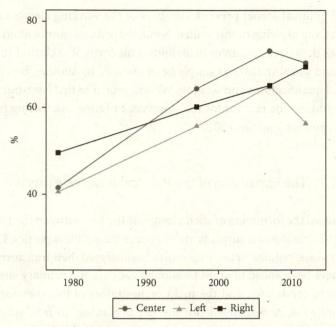

Figure 1.1 Mean time spent in politics as a percentage of adult life, by election year.

In 1978, Left-wing MPs had spent an average of 41% of their adult life in politics (paid positions, elected or not).

to those commonly expected of an elected representative. The waiting line that has formed in front of them forces the new arrivals to wait their turn, at least for a while. The line may be more or less explicit, more or less organized, but it constitutes a principle of selection that is almost impossible to avoid entirely. For people arriving from outside it is therefore very difficult to gain power rapidly, even if they have significant economic or social resources. It is the sign of a field gaining more autonomy and valorizing its own capital over that of other spaces. In Pierre Bourdieu's terminology, it means that any external capital is broadly devalued in favor of sources of value that are produced within the political field.[11]

And as we shall see in Chapter 5, this has many consequences, some of them unexpected. For instance, it makes it more difficult for dignitaries to access politics: elites can no longer be parachuted in the heart of political life (or not as much as before). But this shift is not altogether democratic. The educational requirements demanded for accessing positions as parliamentary aides (which constitute, as we have seen, an effective path to accessing the national political scene) prevent members of the working classes and their children from aspiring to this milieu. Some individuals cannot afford to wait in line, as they need resources or stability. One form of exclusion (based on money and social status) has simply been replaced by another, based on educational qualifications and waiting. We will return to this later, but we now need to address the reasons for the emergence of time as a sorting principle to access politics—up until 2017.

The Expansion of the Political Reserve Army

What caused the formation of such a long waiting line between the 1970s and the 2010s? The obvious suspects are of course the political parties. Over the last forty years, political science literature has analyzed their transformations, which have been substantial. But although they are the primary site for the selection of candidates, and the main orchestrators of this transformation, parties may not be responsible for the rise in waiting. In fact, although all parties are affected in similar ways, the principle of this transformation is probably external to them, that is it lies in the social and political ecosystem in which they are embedded. It is even quite likely that this waiting line to access political positions stems from a larger, structural change. In this area, one of the major transformations of the French political field has to do with the increasing number of politicians and the growing division of labor. Observers of French political scene have noted that, starting in the 1970s, the number of paid political positions grew sharply. In three decades, the number of elected positions rose still further. The number of MPs increased slightly, both in the House (from 482 in 1962 to 577 after 1986), and in the Senate (from 264 in 1964 to 348 after 2011). After the 1980s other elected positions were also created and a series of measures were passed to ensure devolution of power in what was then a very centralized country. Mayors, once of little relevance in comparison to prefects (the representative of the government authority at the local level), were granted more power.

The main change, however, happened not in the number of elected positions, but in the exponential growth of the numbers of staffers. Before 1975 (for the National Assembly) and 1976 (for the Senate) these collaborator positions simply did not exist. MPs only had their "secretaries" to help them with the abundant correspondence they received, but they also shared them with half a dozen other MPs. The rest of the work was solitary, or done collectively by representatives themselves. This started to change in the late 1970s, when MPs were allowed to hire one, then two, and later, in the 2000s, three or more aides each. Unsurprisingly, the number of parliamentary assistants increased constantly during that period. There are now over 2,000 in the National Assembly, and over 1,000 in the Senate.

The same has happened with virtually all other elected positions in France. At the end of the 2000s, researchers found that there were around 7,500 individuals working in the entourage of politicians without being themselves elected (Demaziere & Le Lidec, 2014). Hired at the discretion of their mentor, these aides spend their daily life in politics, and are in a prime position to embark on a political career. In her research about youth political movements, sociologist Lucie Bargel showed how instrumental these positions are for giving young recruits a taste for politics. Far from the all-too-frequently repeated trope that most of those who enter politics do so according to well-established career plans, her careful investigation revealed quite the opposite, that this taste for politics is acquired progressively. Politically motivated but still uncertain about their future upon their arrival in the organization in their late teens, they progressively see politics as a possible, and then as a desirable future for themselves. For them, the waiting period is also the time when their expectations progressively evolve; from being unthinkable, a career in politics gradually became a possibility, and for some a dream, and then a goal (Bargel, 2011).

However, it would be correct to assume that despite their "recent" creation, these positions already existed, at least partly, in another form. In fact, parliamentary archives reveal the existence of staffers before 1975. They were paid by the MP from their personal funds, before special credits for hiring aides were introduced. Other intermediary positions were also available. This was particularly the case within partisan media (newspapers, magazines), a sector that was still flourishing until the 1970s and which was home to individuals working as journalists but who could, either later on or at the same time, move into a political career. The communist newspaper *L'Humanité*, or the former Gaullist paper *La Nation*, served as launching pads for many a politician. For instance, Jean-Luc Mélenchon, until recently the leader of the France Insoumise (and before that a long-time member of the center-left Parti Socialiste), was previously a journalist for one of the party's monthly magazines, *La Tribune du Jura*.

The existence of these elected and nonelected entry-level positions in politics may not be radically new, but since at least the 1970s a twofold change has occurred. First, the number of positions steeply increased. Where there were previously only a few dozen of them, there are now many more paid positions in politics than there used to be. Second, and more significantly, virtually all of these positions are today officially political. Previously, journalists or secretaries who found themselves working in these positions may have been interested in politics, but they also had the possibility of pursuing a career in the company that had initially hired them. They had a foot in two professional worlds and were not necessarily intent on moving into politics. The reverse is quite true today. Having been in politics all their professional lives, some even wonder what would become of them if they were to lose their job.

This structural evolution is probably the primary foundation of the transformation of political careers that France has seen in recent decades. The creation of positions working alongside MPs on the one hand and the prohibition of any private funding on the other (in the wake of the different laws passed after the 1980s, effectively prohibiting the hiring of aides paid by private companies, which was previously a common practice) led to the formation of groups who were actively and primarily involved in politics. As well as acquiring the codes and knowledge of this sphere, they came to enjoy it, and went on to pursue this career for themselves when it became possible for them to do so.

An international comparison would undoubtedly show that this phenomenon is far from specific to France. In Great Britain for example, "special advisors" (also known as "spads") have become increasingly important in national politics. After a stint in a ministerial cabinet, where they hone their skills, many of them to go on to embrace a career in politics. In their book *Special Advisors*, Ben Yong and Robert Hazell (2014) show how these political appointees have become central in Whitehall, with numbers and influence increasing since the 1970s. Some important frontbenchers (among others Edward Miliband and David Cameron) served as spads before they became MPs. In Canada and in New Zealand, the same phenomenon happened, sometimes in larger proportions.

The United States might seem like a counterexample to this. The number of staffers is particularly large in Congress and even larger in the Senate, varying between 30 and 50 per delegate (DeGregorio, 1995). At every other level, even the most local, a whole sector related to politics has developed. Roles like political consulting, communication, publicity, polls, campaigning, or voter registration are not only activities carried out by parties and candidates but also occupations performed by professionals and specialized firms.

Since the 1970s, a real professional sector has emerged (Kavanagh, 1995; Laurison, 2022), and thousands of politicos gravitate around elected officials, in Washington or in the State capitols. In terms of structure, the field is both diverse and made up of thousands of individuals.

Yet, in the US case there were no substantial signs of the early career entry into politics by people who would wait to access national roles. Congressmen and congresswomen do sometimes climb the ladder, but waiting is not the main factor in accessing positions. In this context, money plays a more important role than time[12] (Cage, 2020). The progressive loosening of the restrictions on funding for electoral campaigns—to the point where there are almost no limits, following the Citizens United ruling by the Supreme Court in 2010—have made money even more important. These financial resources may not come from the delegate themselves, as they may have the support of a party or, more often, businesses or personal networks, but money is so crucial that a staffer, a specialist in political communication, or a campaign organizer has next to no chance of becoming a candidate, so there is little point even dreaming about it. In other words, in the US context, proximity with MPs, knowledge of the rules of the game, as well as the acquisition of a strong taste for the political sphere are not enough. There are other, very concrete barriers to playing—the ability to raise several tens of thousands of dollars for even a local campaign being one of them. This means the top rungs of the US political ladder are monopolized by those with money (Carnes, 2020). Such a remark does not invalidate the structural hypothesis according to which the waiting line was created as an extension of the political reserve. But structure is not enough, and the additional barriers of money or celebrity must also be taken into account.

2017, a Populist Moment for the French Elites?

The existence of this political reserve army, the profound transformation of the pathways to national politics, and the general closure of the political field onto itself all played a central role in Macron's victory. It contributed to the sentiment that politics had been hijacked, that it had become the playground of a select few. This image of a world behind closed doors explains much of the appeal of Macron's campaign. His repeated criticisms of career politicians hit a nerve among many voters, who could not help but notice that today's political representatives are the same as they have always been. By resorting to such rhetoric, Macron's tactic fell (somewhat unintentionally) within the scope of a global and increasingly powerful movement to "kick out the incumbents," that was popular in many countries at the time.

The 2017 French elections came after a series of others around the world that saw candidates elected on the theme of radical change, and above all a change in politicians. In Argentina, the slogan, ¡Que se vayan todos! (All of them out!) emerged during protests against the political class in the context of the debt crisis of the early 2000s that plunged the country into unemployment and poverty. It was taken up by opposing parties demanding a massive change of those in political power, who were seen as corrupt, incapable, or both. These demands were echoed across Europe after 2010, and across the political spectrum. On the left they created space for a party like Podemos in Spain, born out of the Indignados movement, which demanded the withdrawal of Spanish political leaders who had been involved in too many corruption and bad management scandals. On the right, the same demands were being voiced in Italy by the self-declared "antisystem" coalition led by the Lega Nord's Matteo Salvini, with the support of Luigi di Maio's Five Star Movement; a coalition that would win power in the 2018 Italian elections.

This was also the case in the United States, with the victory of Donald Trump in the November 2016 presidential election. The latter also based his campaign largely on the criticism of the current political class. It began with attacks against his own party members during the Republican primaries. Jeb Bush, the son and brother of former presidents was, for example, criticized for being part of a dynasty that Trump accused of contributing to the country's decline. Nor did Trump spare Senator Ted Cruz (Texas) and Senator Marco Rubio (Florida), his major adversaries during the primary, accusing them of being part of the system that had led the country into disarray. Once his nomination was ensured, he turned his attacks explicitly on Washington itself, a symbol of political power. With his slogan "drain the swamp" and his proposal to limit the number of terms for legislative representatives, his campaign was clearly that of an outsider, a persona he would continue to cultivate during his term.

At first glance, En Marche! seems quite removed from these movements. The party is socially and economically liberal and defends positions that appear directly opposed to these antisystem parties, some of which advocate protectionism, others national preference. In fact, En Marche! and Macron did explicitly oppose such parties on several occasions, calling them "populists." In the French context, the accusation was geared toward

En Marche!'s two most direct opponents—Marine Le Pen's Rassemblement National and Jean-Luc Mélenchon's La France Insoumise. En Marche! posed itself as the torchbearer of a self-proclaimed "progressivism" against the evils of "populism." The opposition was even theorized by two advisors to the president. In a book that set out to present the principles of the centrist philosophy En Marche! aimed to embody, the authors defended the idea that the key opposition in this election was not between the "left" and the "right" (which Macron claimed to transcend), but between "populism" and "progressivism."[13]

Yet it seems that Macron's party benefited from the same conditions that saw a surge in these "populists" during the 2010s. This is another illustration of the situation described above where Macron and his team cleverly took advantage of a situation that was beyond their control. The clearest example of this is undoubtedly the criticism of the "professionalization of politics" that was used throughout the whole En Marche! campaign and which was only ever a more polished version of the same denunciation of all politicians that is typical of so-called populist parties. It is difficult to ignore the fact that the "populist" mood criticized by En Marche! in fact served it very well.

We could even go further and argue that Macron's party is in fact an example—atypical, but not ultimately that different—of the very same species against which it claims to fight. For this, we need to return to the definitions of this phenomena. The term "populism" is a conflictual one, according to its main theorist Cas Mudde. It is often used as an insult rather than as a descriptive adjective and above all it serves to confer certain vague but exclusively negative characteristics (Mudde & Kaltwasser, 2013). If we try to cast it in a more positive light, several elements emerge. First, if we follow Mudde, populism is a "thin" ideology, flexible, and compatible with very different ideological discourses—whether pro- or anti-immigration, or pro- or anti–financial markets. The long list of parties and situations that fall into the populist category is a sign of its lack of ideological coherence as a category, although the authors consider it a worthwhile term.

Moreover, there are three characteristics that emerge from a comparison between different movements that are regularly described as populist. The first is the personalization of power. According to Mudde and his followers, populist movements share a promotion of an individual rather than an organization, an individualization of politics, and the figure of a charismatic leader (i). The second characteristic is a rejection of the current elites. These may be economic and financial elites, as was the case in the Occupy Wall

Street movement, or they may be political elites. There is also a frequent trend toward "*dégagisme*"[14] (removing incumbents) (ii). The third characteristic is the reliance on the "general will" or even "the people's wisdom" as the central decision-making principal, rather than on representative democracy. Representation is in fact considered the source of many contemporary ills (oligarchy, power mongering, etc.) that the return to popular decision-making is thought to alleviate (iii).

If we accept, even temporarily, this definition of populism, it would be difficult to deny that En Marche! falls into this category—at least in a diluted way. As we have seen, it is a movement organized around the figure of Emmanuel Macron, in a party whose initials matched his. The long refusal by En Marche! to adopt a clear platform is another sign of personalization, where the individual plays a more important role than what he stands for. It is also important to not forget that political platforms gained footing across Europe in the late 19th century, when republicans tried to unseat the monarchists, in large part the nobility, who wished to run on their name and reputation alone. Macron even went further, explicitly casting himself as a savior figure. In May 2017, he drew a parallel between himself and Joan of Arc, evoking a "wild dream [to break away from the system] that became obvious, self-evident."[15] In February of the same year he reiterated his criticism of campaign platforms and declared that "it is a mistake to believe the platform is the heart of the campaign [. . .] politics is mystical." In this way, he declared he wanted to "intertwine intelligence and spirituality," before implicitly accepting "the Christ-like dimension" of his action.[16]

The second aspect of Mudde's definition—the rejection of political elites—is also clearly present in the movement during both campaigns. Of course this was a limited criticism and did not extend to the sphere of power as a whole—cynics might say such a line would have been too dangerous for a party that essentially recruited among the social and economic elites—but it was a strong theme nonetheless. In the end, it is only En Marche!'s position on representative democracy that did not fit Mudde's typology of populist movements. The party very clearly situated itself within the institutional frame of the Fifth Republic, and just as clearly promoted elections as a method of democratic expression. But even in this case, Macron and his teams were at best ambivalent in their position if we consider the fact that representative democracy is not just a series of legal frameworks, but also an ensemble of institutions that ensure the involvement of citizens in political life. From this perspective, En Marche's criticism of parties as an intermediary is not so removed from other claims by populist parties. And in fact, Macron said exactly that when he refused the idea of formal mediation, a position shared by many leaders accused of populism: "if being populist means wanting to engage with the people without going through the [party or union] apparatuses, I'm happy to be called a populist."[17]

The positions that brought Macron and his party to power in 2017 could be debated at length, as could the question of whether they are populist, and even the nature of populism itself and whether it is suitable to describe contemporary (French) politics. But pausing to reflect on the proximity between En Marche! and what it has constructed as its negative other, is a reminder that it cannot be seen as an alternative to populism. At best, it expressed a diluted form of populism *during the election season*. It shows how Macron's party rode the same wave of discontent against politicians that saw a surge in these "populists" during the 2010s. His criticism of the "professionalization of politics" was only ever a more polished version of the same denunciation of the political class that is typical of so-called populist parties.

This is a clear illustration of a situation where Macron and his team cleverly took advantage of a broader climate. But this was not the only instance of this efficient opportunism. To claim the presidency, against all odds, with the support of a small outsider party, created less than a year before the election, Macron had to navigate contingencies and make the most of them. Of course, his campaign encountered many surprises along the way.

A Brutal Reconfiguration

2017, an Atypical Campaign?

Academics, journalists, and political commentators alike have emphasized the exceptional nature of the 2017 electoral season. It is true that although political campaigns are always unpredictable to a certain extent, they often result in relatively predictable outcomes. But not in 2017, where the campaign was marked by a series of events that were impossible to foresee, and the result was highly improbable.

Ordinarily, François Hollande, as the incumbent president of the French Republic, would have been an obvious candidate for his own succession. But he did not run. His time in office was difficult, marked by terrorist attacks, unwaveringly high unemployment, and reforms that were considered both unpopular and insufficient. The second part of his mandate was marked by opposition from within his own political family. A proposal to strip terrorists of French nationality sparked immense controversy within the left. Later, he introduced a composite bill aiming to reform certain aspects of France's labor code, which led to substantial protest movements. The brutal police response to these protests led to a schism between the Socialist Party, its left-wing allies, and some of its supporters. Against the backdrop of these tensions, a new parliamentary movement, as unprecedented as it was substantial, emerged and divided the majority. This schism, known as "la Fronde" (the revolt)—a reference to the French civil wars of the 17th century that erupted during the Franco-Spanish conflict—made it harder for the government to pass some of the legislation it wished to. This pushback against the government clearly contributed to the erosion of Hollande's status as the natural leader of the Socialist Party, as well as his support from his electorate. On December 1, 2016, having been forced to accept the principle of a primary in his own political camp, he renounced his candidacy for re-election, even though it had been planned and organized since his first day in office.

These primaries also did not have the same effect as they had had in the past, when they had successfully brough the Socialist Party and its supporters together around a clear, consensual, candidate. This time, they led to the nomination of the most left-wing candidate on offer, Benoît Hamon, who would quickly be criticized. He was a long-time party activist, former leader of the youth wing of the party and a central player in "la Fronde." He was also the head of a faction within the party that was seen as having positions that were out of step with the dominant social-liberal line the party had defended for at least a decade.

In a mirror-like effect, the newly adopted primaries yielded similarly surprising results on the political right. Here, an internal election was organized to choose between three candidates, each of whom had a solid party background: former president Nicolas Sarkozy, and two former ministers, Alain Juppé and François Fillon. The primary was open to all voters, as it had been on the left, but this time a whopping 4 million voters participated. Defying all odds, François Fillon won the second round hands down over Alain Juppé in November 2016—Sarkozy having been eliminated in the first round. Once again, if we use the left-right scale as a guide, the winning candidate was the one furthest from the central position of the party. Indeed, Fillon had based his campaign on traditional moral values, evoking his "personal doubts" regarding abortion (an otherwise consensual topic in the French political field), and "personally disapproving" of same-sex marriage, a rarely contested piece of legislation at the time. In other words, he was significantly more conservative than the median positions of his party.

These primaries on both the left and the right were in Macron's favor, ensuring he had no direct competitor for the center of the political space—his core target. Moreover, the left-wing candidate Hamon was rapidly abandoned by a segment of his party, and on the right, Fillon struggled to get his campaign off the ground. Then came the allegations that during his time as an MP—nearly thirty years—François Fillon had paid his wife to work as a staffer, a job no one could remember her doing, neither in the party nor at the Assemblée. After the initial revelations were published in the satirical investigative newspaper the *Canard Enchaîné* in January 2017, not a week went by without new discoveries of indiscretions hampering his campaign. His press conferences, public events, and anything he organized in the field were all swamped by this subject. The situation was all the more complicated because he had promoted himself as a man of honor, and his campaign was built on financial rigor and careful budgetary spending. As a self-proclaimed herald of moral righteousness, he saw his main argument, his integrity, whittled away week by week. Despite increasing pressure from within his party, Fillon remained the official candidate of the right and the center, while a portion of his supporters and his electorate shifted toward Emmanuel Macron.

External circumstances thus facilitated Macron's candidacy immensely. But to focus only on these events raises the risk of obscuring all the actions—both his and those of his team—that made this result possible. Far from simply being a product of circumstance, the plausibility of Macron's candidacy was based as much on the way he and his team constructed it, and adjusted it to his circumstances, or indeed were able to create those circumstances. From this point of view, the 2017 campaign was less abnormal, and the strategies adopted during it were ultimately quite typical.

The beginnings of Macron's campaign are often traced back to Spring 2016. In April of that year, he created a new microparty, a structure intended to support a future candidacy, although he told his government colleagues and the media that it would be his contribution to the campaign of the incumbent president's future campaign. En Marche! would be "a satellite of the Socialist Party," rather than a competitor. At the same time, he launched the organization of his own campaign. In June, En Marche! decided to organize a "Long March"; its activists, transformed into impromptu interviewers, were sent out to collect information through questionnaires on the concerns of French voters. The results were analyzed quantitatively with a view to revealing the deep issues relevant to French voters. It was also meant to preempt a criticism Macron worried he would be targeted with, given his background—that he was out of touch with the problems of ordinary citizens.

This action, and others, were made possible by the financial resources that Macron had at his disposal from very early on. Money should have been an issue for him. Because he had not been involved in previous campaigns, Macron was not able to access to the public funding most of his opponents received. This could also not be compensated for via private donation, since the restrictions on campaign funding are quite strict in France, and have been since the 1990s. In addition to public resources, the main parties are only allowed to receive money from private individuals—not companies—within certain limits. For a presidential election, the main parties generally manage to mobilize around 20 million euros each for their candidate, this sum being the upper limit for a presidential campaign (Cage, 2020). The amount may pale in comparison to the expenses of a presidential election in other countries, especially in the United States, but nevertheless, this budget constitutes a significant barrier for any potential candidate without party support.[18]

But here too, the soon-to-be-candidate's team was busy collecting the first donations, as early as April 2016 (Offerlé, 2019). The "Macron Leaks," a trove of emails hacked from the campaign team and published two days before the second round of the elections, revealed a very effective strategy that had been put in place to establish a party treasury. Even though Macron himself had no money, his supporters had some. Substantial donations were paid into the party coffers early on, allowing him to launch various initiatives and to hire some staff. By late 2016, the movement had collected more than 5 million euros in private donations (less than the 7.5 million collected by the right-wing Républicains, but significantly more than the Socialist Party candidate). Moreover, the finance and taxation law knowledge of several campaign members were rapidly put to good use. As political scientist Rémi Lefebvre noted, "overall, more than 10 million euros were donated by individuals," which is an enviable amount for French political parties (Lefebvre, 2019). Unsurprisingly, most of them were wealthy donors.

Macron's party would eventually produce a campaign platform just like the other parties. For several months, however, the candidate refused the idea of a program at all. The proclaimed desire to break with traditional frameworks of the political field led him to refuse what he saw as a symbol of the "system" he was up against. He even went so far as to explicitly express this refusal, saying, "a program with 300 intended measures is absolutely meaningless," or "I am sorry to tell you that we don't give a shit about party programs!"[19] Yet the program was being written behind the scenes. It was eventually presented, in February 2017, and it was ultimately quite traditional—it matched all the requirements of the contemporary "programmatic" genre (Fertikh, 2020). Ironically enough, it ended up being even longer than Macron's predecessors' programs.[20]

In less than a year, Macron had gone from being unimaginable as a candidate, to being a plausible one, and eventually being elected president. The solution to this political conundrum can be found in the particular combination of circumstances and specific resources contributed by a social class that mobilized around his candidacy.[21] Macron gained credibility from the positive dynamic produced through this configuration of circumstances; although the polls were initially not promising, they improved in the autumn. Always under careful scrutiny by observers, these polls helped shift his status as a candidate over time, and thus his ability to influence the political field. After a period of waiting patiently, January brought a wave of allegiances from a handful of politicians, followed by still more in March, when MPs from both parties as well as incumbent government ministers officially came out in support of his candidacy.

Realignments

To fully understand Macron's success, we must consider the dynamics between action, individual and collective, and the political structure in which it takes place. This is where Bourdieusian analysis in terms of field is useful, as it allows to consider these aspects together. Adopting this relational approach has one clear advantage. It allows us to understand how an individual, somewhat of an outsider to the field, was able to progressively impose his rhythm onto the political field and force his competitors to respond to his every move. If we are to understand how Macron successfully set himself up as a plausible, and subsequently obvious solution after initially being ignored, we must first understand how he became what Bourdieu calls a nomothetic figure, the person that prescribes norms that constrains others, who then have to position themselves in relation to them.

This power to dictate the pace of the field, which was obvious in the last months of the campaign, was even more visible after the election. In May, Macron's status changed and discussions became structured around his

48   THE CANDIDATES

proposals. Many signs demonstrated this throughout this year. A surprising one is that Macron's name, his image, and his party were used broadly and sometimes unexpectedly during the legislative campaign. Many candidates—whether or not they had the party's official support, and regardless of their own political family—came out in support of the presidential party. On their posters, on their leaflets, they more or less obviously claimed to belong to the presidential party—for instance with phrases like "with the presidential majority" adorning the campaign posters. In a few instances, these slogans even appeared on the posters of half of the candidates in a given constituency. Posters also frequently used the same kind of graphics and colors as the presidential party. The one presented below provide concrete examples of this kind of borrowing. Some reappropriated the name of the party, En marche!, others used the same slogan, or imitated it closely. One of the candidates also kept the distinctive font used by En Marche! Blue and yellow, the colors of the party, were dominant, and party logos from other movements were often minimized or removed altogether. Likewise, the candidates' statements and programs were also used as a space to announce their "support" of the new president.

Campaign posters for the 2017 legislative elections

This situation is not unusual in itself, but it was more visible than in the past electoral years. What made this campaign remarkable is that high-profile leaders of *other parties* also used the same strategy. For these highly visible candidates it was impossible to conceal the fact that they were not in the presidential party, that they had not been early supporters of the new president, and that they had not officially received its support. Some had even publicly opposed Macron before his election. Yet their posters closely resemble the examples above. The most obvious example of this is the poster of the former socialist prime minister, Manuel Valls. In his constituency of Evry, in the Parisian suburbs, he ran a hotly contested campaign to retain his seat in Parliament. As prime minister, Valls had challenged Macron several times when the latter was Minister for Economics, and as head of government, even tried to limit his room to maneuver. This did not prevent him from campaigning with a poster that was very close to that of the République en Marche, and which even mentioned the "presidential majority." Marisol Touraine, who was then still minister for health in the socialist government, went even further. Her poster in the first round, along with the rest of her electoral material, explicitly mentioned the name of the president and support that may not have been reciprocated. The distinctive colors of the République en Marche, blue and yellow, were omnipresent, but the traditional red of the Socialist Party was altogether absent. In fact, on the posters of both Valls and Touraine, the PS party logo had disappeared entirely.

Campaign posters for the 2017 legislative elections

Although rare, this situation is not unprecedented in French history. It even resembles the context in which de Gaulle returned to power in 1958, at a time of military tension and potential civil war. The then French president, René Coty, called on General de Gaulle, celebrated for his role in the Resistance, to take up the role of President of the Conseil (similar to today's prime minister). Elections were held in November, after the September referendum which had validated the regime change. Although de Gaulle was not intensely involved in the election, his aura combined with the discredit of his opponents saw the political leaders of the outgoing regime drop party labels and try to promote their closeness to de Gaulle. At the time, many candidates who did not belong to his party tried to distance themselves from the world of politics. Some removed the party logo from their posters or followed the same graphic style of his poster. And when it was impossible to conceal the fact that they were opponents, they emphasized the local issues of the election. Their campaign statements stressed their biographical trajectory rather than their party affiliations. Their original trades and professions were presented at length (even when they had been in politics for years) as a way of demonstrating a connection to the world outside politics. As political scientist Brigitte Gaïti wrote of the 1958 legislative elections, "almost everyone was hiding behind the Gaullist screen and either denounced their opponents as professional politicians, or presented themselves in ways that were less directly political" (Gaïti, 1999).

All these elements suggest that success was not purely a matter of chance, nor was it down to the individual skills mobilized on the path to victory. Both of these things were undeniably important, but insufficient, in accounting for the result—that is, the partial disorganization and then the abrupt reconstruction of the political field around the figure of Emmanuel Macron. To a certain extent, he had successfully taken up the position of the "prophet," in the sense that sociologist Max Weber gives to the term. In his work on religion, Weber identifies several actors that typically compete against each other to increase their followership. The "priest" is the representative of the institution, and he receives his authority directly from it. He has skills (liturgical literacy, knowledge of the rites) and competences acquired through education. He also represents and enforces the orthodoxy. The "prophet," by contrast, does not get his authority from the institution—in fact, he is trying to subvert it. But he speaks the same language, often has the same codes, and just promotes an alternative orthodoxy—a new system against the old one. This position is much more likely to succeed than that of the third type of actor, the "magician," who only promotes local solutions and does not claim to replace the existing system.

In this sense, Macron was the ultimate figure of the prophet, as he combined a deep knowledge of the political field but promoted an alternative offer that appeared radical to many. Upon launching his bid for president, Macron had qualifications that made him a perfectly legitimate—if somewhat young—presidential candidate in the eyes of many commentators and supporters. He was a graduate of Sciences Po and the École Nationale d'Administration, and he was a former member of the prestigious Inspection des finances (Inspectorate General of France), one of France's highest administrative positions, obtained after yet another competitive exam. Although he had never been elected before, he had been in politics or very close to it, on several occasions. In the years before he ran, he was a deputy chief of staff for the French president, and a prominent minister. Overall, his trajectory was ultimately very typical, although quite rapid.

Yet at the same time he expressed his distance from the political sphere. This act of conspicuous rejection enabled him to capitalize on the criticism of the system that he claimed to transform, while retaining the legitimacy it bestowed upon him. And since he had embarked on the presidential race without party backing, he could hardly claim a connection with the parties. He nonetheless made the best of the situation by presenting the parties as his opponents, thus reinforcing his claim of exteriority. With all the qualifications to make himself a credible candidate but unsullied by an attachment to the "system" that he was of course deeply familiar with, the young president seemed the embodiment of an impossible combination. Throughout the campaign, Macron subtly played on these two apparently irreconcilable characteristics, successfully combining them to cast himself as a providential man—striving against the evils of political professionalization.

His endeavor appeared destined for success, because as well as becoming president, his mandate would see the most significant "renewal" of parliament in the long history of the Fifth Republic. But would this bring about the fundamental change he had announced? Or would the renewal be mere show? The next chapter will set out to provide an answer.

2
A PALACE WAR, NOT A REVOLUTION

"We're farmers, painters, athletes, or mathematicians. We are students, self-employed, or retirees. For some of us, it's our first time in politics. Others have been elected before. We're on the march [a play on words with En marche!] because we feel like we aren't being represented by career politicians who have been in power for decades. We're on the march because it is time to revitalize political life."[1] This is the voice-over from the ad campaign launched by Macron's party for the June elections. Spoken as portraits of candidates posing as everyday citizens appeared on the screen, this spiel perfectly captures the image the party wanted to convey about itself at that moment, as socially and politically diverse, giving pride of place to young people and minorities, and made up of equal numbers of men and women. The movement tried to spin an image of itself as the exact opposite of the established political class—depicted as old, white, and male. Barely a month later, more than 60% of these candidates were elected.

In some respects, that campaign promise of diversity was kept. With over 72% of MPs elected for the first time—compared to an average of around 33% ordinarily—the 15th legislature that began in June 2017 was unlike any other. Even back in 1958, after General de Gaulle returned to power in the midst of a profound political crisis, only 68% of elected MPs were newcomers. Other indicators show that the change in 2017 was massive. The legislature welcomed an unprecedented number of women (39% compared to 25% in the immediately preceding terms), it also ushered in large numbers of young people, and dozens of genuine political novices. Moreover, all of these changes were essentially brought about by the victory of La République en Marche and publicized by the "movement"—a term used during the campaign, to accentuate their difference from traditional parties. The "new faces of parliament" were presented as the embodiment of this "new world" the party wanted to see emerge.

It did not take long, though, for this narrative to be called into question. Some observers argued that some those ushered in under the "civil society" banner had in fact been in politics for a long time in various capacities—often as long-term activists, union leaders, or political staffers. This was a far cry from the image of "novices" the party claimed. Critics also mentioned that for all the positive publicity around the new "Assemblée," one central fact was never mentioned—its social elitism. After all, the vast majority of the MPs were from upper-class backgrounds, and even more so within the ranks of La République en Marche, the new name adopted by En Marche! after the elections (abbreviated to the acronym LREM).

In the end, this 2017 legislature gave rise to many remarks, few of them neutral. Depending on their political leaning, on the evidence available to them, or the angle they had adopted, commentators emphasized one angle over others. As with any interpretation, they tended to obscure the elements that did not match their narrative. By contrast, this chapter aims to provide a comprehensive perspective of this new legislature. Using original and extensive data about the professional and political careers of MPs in France, the purpose here is to better assess the change that happened in 2017, but also to identify the trends that survived this massive change, and those that were reinforced.

This deep dive into the data reveals that there was indeed a renewal in 2017. Individuals who were unlikely to become MPs before, found themselves thrust onto the national political scene. Before the campaign, back in January, many of these MPs could not have imagined that they would get involved in politics. In March they were involved but would not have dreamed of running as a candidate; by May they were candidates but still did not think they would be elected. Nevertheless, in June they found themselves on the benches of the Lower House. However, this research also demonstrates that the change was both less strong and less systemic than it seemed. Not only was the number of genuine novices ultimately smaller than the nearly 50% claimed by the presidential party, but in many respects the 2017 assembly was no more representative of French society than the previous ones—and in some areas it was less so.

But there is more. Quantitative data, along with interviews, clearly show that Macron's victory made it possible for countless MPs to get around the line they had been waiting in, and directly access national political positions, to essentially "jump the queue." This is particularly true for many who were already involved in politics, as running mates or as staffers. More than anything else, they managed to speed up their career. Like Macron himself, they profited from the general misgivings against the "old world" and ran for nomination, with success. As a result, over the course of just a few months, their careers were accelerated. In the end, the "revolution" Macron called for in his campaign book of 2016 by the same name, looked more like palace infighting. Rather than providing a complete turnover, for many already in politics, 2017 was a great shortcut.

Changes in the House

New Kids on the Floor

The end of each parliamentary recess is a delicate moment for the ushers of the National Assembly. These officials, easily recognizable in their traditional black livery decorated with a silver chain, are responsible for the smooth functioning of the lower house. The most well-known chamber of the French Parliament, the *hémicycle*, as it is known, is also a restricted space where these ushers control both entry and movement. They convey messages to the MPs and bring them food and drink. They may also physically intervene when tensions run high.

Although not strictly speaking on their job description, there is another quality that is required to hold this prestigious position. Parliamentary ushers must also be excellent at physiognomy. Recognizing faces is an important skill because after the first few days, not many of the MPs wear their badges, and they do not take kindly to being asked for identification. From this perspective, French voters made their life complicated when they voted in 430 new MPs—radically changing the face of the Assembly. The percentage of new MPs in this legislature was unprecedented under the Fifth Republic. It meant that an intense summer revision was in order for the ushers, the discrete officials responsible for access to and movement around the *hémicycle*.

But beyond its superficial "face" change, was the National Assembly genuinely different? In order to answer this question, we can look at the sociodemographic properties of those within it; indeed, this is often the first thing social and political scientists do. In these disciplines, the study of characteristics of elected representatives is a genre in itself, with a long-standing tradition. But it is also closely examined by journalists, civic groups, and even political parties concerned about the public image of their candidates. Many try to read the signs of future decisions in the biography of the elected members. One must nonetheless be careful. The omnipresent reliance on biography all too often conceals the diversity of criteria investigated. As

French political scientist Frédéric Sawicki noted, the apparent simplicity of the compilation of biographical details "raises the question of what counts, and how it should be counted" (1999, p. 165). For example, the social portrait produced by this an investigation into politicians' characteristics will differ significantly depending on whether the focus is on the MP's occupation immediately prior to election, on the one they held the longest, or on their parents' professions. Any number of examples could be given here.

The results also differ depending on whether the analysis is based on an indicator chosen and coded by the researcher, or if the latter has to rely solely on declarations by MPs. With the rise of digital data, it is now easy to collect large amounts of information about MPs listed on different websites, including their own and that of the institution. But as we have already noted, these are hardly reliable, past the most basic information such as age, place, and date of birth. The reason for this is simple. Given that these websites often constitute the most immediately available information about MPs, the latter are very careful that they present themselves in as flattering a light as possible. This is particularly true for occupations. Given the stigma associated with a long-term presence in politics in the beginning of the 21st century, many MPs emphasize the aspects of their trajectory that show a connection to the outside world—even if they were very brief. Research thus cannot be based on these self-declarations. If we want to study parliamentary trajectories, bias can be avoided, but at the cost of careful and sometimes painstaking research. This is what we set out to achieve in the project I conducted with Sébastian Michon and Julien Boelaert, some elements of which have been published elsewhere.[2] This meticulous analysis of MPs' careers provides a precise and detailed portrait of the 15th legislature, which was clearly quite unique.

The percentage of first-time MPs is just one aspect of the changes that this new legislature brought about. As in 1958, when the political class were brutally dismissed in circumstances that were not dissimilar, 2017 saw the arrival of individuals with profiles that were unusual in the political sphere. This is particularly clear in terms of gender. The French parliament, like so many others around the world, is characterized by the underrepresentation of women. Overall, between 1958 and 2012, 94% of French MPs were men,[3] a figure that has now dropped only to 90%. This imbalance is also verified in terms of flows. The percentage of women in parliament rose from 4% before 1981, to 6% between 1981 and 1993, but it did not reach 10% until the 11th legislature (1997–2002), later increasing to 25% in 2012. In this sense, 2017 brought a substantial change in parliament, with a whopping 39% of MPs being women. This percentage even reached 50% among the ranks of LREM itself, making it the first governing party to enforce real gender parity. This change was all the more remarkable in that France has never been at the forefront of gender equality in politics. By comparison, the Swedish legislature elected in 2014 was 44% women, that of 2018 48%. Quasi-perfect gender parity may be a Scandinavian exception but other countries did better. There were 39% women in the Belgian parliament in 2014 and the same proportion in Spain in 2015. In Denmark, 37% of the parliament was made up of women in 2015, and in Germany the figure was 30% for 2017 and 35% in 2021.

This kind of shift can also be seen in terms of age. During the Fifth Republic, French MPs were generally around 50 years old, but in the lower house, this average has tended to increase in recent years. In 1959, on average MPs were elected at age 49, a figure that increased steadily to reach 56 in 2012. In 2017, it suddenly dropped back down to 49. This average also conceals a broad distribution, several very young MPs were elected in 2017 (in their th30sirties or even younger). Delegates this young were extremely rare in previous legislatures.

This influx of much younger MPs caused problems for the parliamentary staff. Not only did they have to learn the faces of all these new first-time MPs very quickly—according to a rumor, some invented ingenious games to memorize their faces more easily—but they also had to be able to distinguish the MP from his or her retinue of collaborators. In this new legislature, a young 30-something man or woman flanked by an older man in a suit, could be the MP and his/her assistant, rather than the other way around. This led to a number of confusions that sociologist Juliette Bresson documented in her interviews with these new arrivals. Some accepted the mistaken identities with good grace, but others got tired of them. One of these legislators told her how he ended up losing his temper one day when, trailed by a journalist, he was asked yet again what he was doing in this particular place (Bresson, 2018, pp. 68–69).

Finally, 2017 saw the average time previously spent in politics drop dramatically. Where in 1978 an MP spent over 18 years on average in politics before being elected (close to 12 for first-time MPs), in 2012, this number dropped to less than 11 years (6.6 for new arrivals). The results are even more striking when expressed as a percentage of working life spent in politics. Where the 2012 MPs were active and in paid political positions for 68% of their adult life, this proportion dropped to 42% in 2017.

Other indicators, mentioned in Table 2.1, also reflect this transformation. The number of MPs who were previously political aides declined (from 33% to 24%), and, conversely, the number of MPs with no past political experience went from 5% to 27%. Although some may have had a very long involvement in politics, the shift was clear; a substantial number of new MPs had not lived off politics before 2017, a situation that was almost unheard of previously.

These changes reflect the message promoted by LREM. They are also heavily influenced by the MPs in this parliamentary group, because with 312 MPs elected in June 2017, the delegates from LREM had a strong impact on these overall statistics. It is true that they were in a particularly favorable

Table 2.1 Indicators of French MPs' political activities prior to election

Legislature	6th	9th	13th	14th	15th
	1978–1981	1997–2002	2007–2012	2012–2017	2017–
Staffer (%)	14.2	23.5	29.4	32.6	23.8
Women	0.0	24.7	23.6	22.8	17.5
Men	14.8	23.4	30.8	36.2	27.7
No previous political position (%)	8.8	1.8	1.1	5.0	27.7
Women	19.0	6.8	2.4	9.0	38.6
Men	8.3	1.2	0.8	3.5	20.7
Percentage of one's career spent in politics (%)	46.0	62.5	70.7	67.6	42.3
Women	32.6	49.1	57.7	51.9	27.4
Men	46.5	64.2	73.9	73.3	51.9
Number of years spent in politics (elected or employed)	12.1	16.5	19.8	18.5	10.6
Women	7.7	12.3	15.7	13.7	6.6
Men	12.3	17.0	20.8	20.3	13.2
Average age at the beginning of the legislature	51.2	52.6	54.9	54.4	49.1
Women	47.5	50.4	53.6	52.9	47.9
Men	51.4	52.9	55.2	55.0	49.9

Note: 23.8% of MPs elected in 2017 were previously staffers, compared to 32.6% of MPs elected in 2012.

situation in this regard because the movement did not have incumbent MPs and thus had fewer constraints in these nominations.

An Original Selection Procedure

These figures partly reflect the work done by the movement in launching these new candidates. From January 2017, En Marche! issued a call for candidates that was almost unprecedented in the history of French political parties—at least for a movement that aspired to govern: it launched a wide, public call for applications. It did so by setting up an Internet site in order to have candidates running in virtually all constituencies. This was successful, given that between 15,000 and 20,000 people applied to be candidates, according to party documents. A selection process was thus organized. This was the task of the national investiture committee, an internal organization made up of nine members who came together twice a week between January and May.

One must keep in mind that this kind of process is very rare. The implicit selection rules and recruitment procedures for candidates vary greatly between parties; some maintain tight control while others simply ratify the choices of local branches. But even in the light of this great variety, the centralization of the investiture committee in LREM was particularly unusual, because in this case all the decisions were made by a very small group of people. The only comparison that comes to mind is the postwar Communist Party in certain European countries. For the Communists, biography was key because it was central to the party's image, which varied over the years. After World War II, the French Communist Party wanted to come across as the party of the Resistance (the party of the "75,000 martyrs," executed by the Nazis). Later, the biographical trait put forward would be occupational, and more specifically a premium would be placed on being a member of the working class. As a result, it retained close control over the choice of candidates, and sometimes tinkered with their biographies to emphasize their more desirable, more authentically blue-collar, characteristics.

The same thing happened in 2017. Probably even more than the French Communist Party in its day, En Marche! established a very centralized selection committee. The selection criteria were made clear. One member of this committee laid out the main elements in an interview:

There were three very specific criteria: [...] gender parity, probity, and political experience. ... On probity, well, we didn't have much data [*on previous convictions*] but we had to keep it in mind, and we checked if there were any incompatibilities with a particular role. [...] But gender parity was especially something we looked at very closely and which also allowed us to add a few more [women].[4]

According to this interviewee, at the beginning of each meeting, the data was checked to make sure these objectives remained within reach as the candidates were selected. Each time there was an imbalance, the choices were readjusted. The statistics quoted above confirm that these criteria (parity, political profile from civil society) were indeed taken into account. There was even an effort made to encourage women candidates:

At the beginning there was a real deficit of women.... I think that we can say that. There was a real deficit of women candidates, so the initial choice was to say that we select, so to say, we select all the women who applied. And that's where Emmanuel Macron's appeal came from. If we wanted to reach parity, there's a basic principle, in terms of stock, we had to have more stock.[5]

A few weeks after the launch of the appeal for candidates, there were still not enough women, so they decided to make a specific appeal, through Emmanuel Macron himself, on International Women's Day.

And that's why there was a huge amount of work done on.... And we're talking about it today, on the 8th of March [the interview took place on International Women's Day], but the work to find women candidates was intense. There was Emmanuel Macron's call, but also work by teams who went to find candidates, to convince them, reassure them, tell them they were capable.[6]

This appeal was then followed by an initiative named "Elles Marchent" (the women march), aimed to encourage women candidates to participate in the process, and to support them throughout it. These attempts were ultimately successful because the movement was able to run male and female candidates at parity in 2017. The procedure itself, which was atypical because based on an online candidacy, undoubtedly helped to bridge the gender gap. In fact, several of the women interviewed afterward admitted they applied "without telling their friends and colleagues," or "without informing members of the party" they were active in. This private process, which was made possible by the combination of technology and a centralized commission, meant they could keep their ambition secret until late in the day, thus avoiding the offhand but powerful discouraging remarks a potential candidate might face every day.

A newly minted MP I interviewed describes this process. In 2012, she had considered running, but she eventually stepped back in the face of the surprised reactions she encountered. These remarks were sometimes disparaging ("Really?," "You, a candidate?"), and repeated with other signals, they had diminished the still fragile faith she had in her legitimacy to run, and eventually discouraged her from applying for candidacy. In 2017 she did, but this time she kept the application process a secret until it was official—something that was allowed by the anonymity of the website. By providing a space for anonymous application, LREM managed—probably unwittingly, but efficiently—to limit the classic processes of self-exclusion that affect minority groups, and primarily women.

Other criteria were less central for the investiture committee. In this same interview, this commission member mentioned in passing the question of MPs' social representativity. According to her, this issue was not avoided, but it was only taken into account with a view to adapting the candidate to the constituency. "There was also a question, which was not so much a public criteria, but that we still paid attention to, which was sociological representativity, which was necessarily geographic." When prompted again on this point later in the interview, she said "it was less of an issue." In other words, the social background of candidates was only taken into account to ensure a better match with the constituency.

The data also confirms a limited interest in social diversity. The House that was elected in 2017—and the LREM group in particular—were clearly different from the French population on average. The data shows this; there is a flagrant lack of workers and employees, the two groups that define the working class, for the French statistics service. While they represent 48% of the French active population, they were only 2% of those elected in 2017. By contrast, the upper classes are well represented in this legislature, even more than they are normally. The LREM group was made up of 60% managers and senior professionals (which constitute just 17.7% of the active population in general). If we add the other category of the French census covering entrepreneurs and small-business owners, the percentage of higher social categories among LREM MPs, increases to 75% compared to 24% in the French population. The 2017 French Lower House was clearly the realm of the bourgeoisie.

This remark about social origins points toward yet another limitation of the discourses on career politicians. The overinsistence on time spent in politics tends to obscure the fact that other equally legitimate forms of classification are neglected when this criterion becomes hegemonic. Of course, it could be objected that previous legislatures were no more representative of French society, and that parliaments are seldom a genuine reflection of the voting population—and still less of the social body more generally. This fact is clear, even though as we will see in Chapter 5, this legislature was probably was the least socially diverse in recent decades. In fact, the French parliament has probably not been this socially homogeneous since the late 19th century. It is also worth noting that despite all the discourse against political professionalization, the sharp decrease in the time spent in politics may not necessarily indicate a "deprofessionalization" of the parliament. To see if what looks like a radical upheaval is more than a sheer career acceleration, we need to look more closely at individual trajectories.

Throw the Bums Out?

The legislative elections of 2017 brought an undeniable, although partial, renewal of the French parliament. It ushered in a lot of new people, some completely unknown to the public. But can this influx—as extensive as it was—be interpreted as a deprofessionalization of French politics? In order to answer that question, we must first ask what professional politics, and politicians, look like. Although this might seem like a simple question, social sciences have as yet failed to provide an unequivocal answer.

Of course, this lack of certainty does not mean there is a lack of research on the subject, merely that the rich existing literature is not conclusive.[7] In British political science, in particular, the question has a long history. Anthony King's article (1981) is often cited and has given rise to a field of research in its own right, with a range of debates and observations. It has also demonstrated the difficulty of measurement. How can we determine precisely what constitutes a "career politician"? Should it refer to anyone paid to work in politics, at a given moment in time? Should it be someone who spends their whole life in various elected mandates? Or, should there be a threshold, in years perhaps, beyond which one indisputably falls into that category? Depending on the criteria selected, the answer to the above question will be very different.

An exchange between British political scientists Philipp Cowley (2012) and Stephen Barber (2014) in the early 2010s illustrates this well. Depending on the reference point adopted, the length of contemporary British political leaders' careers could be regarded as either long, or on the contrary very short. And depending on this measure, the interpretation of the phenomenon changed drastically. The growing interest in academia also had an unintended, albeit highly predictable, consequence: it made it fuzzier. Writing about the topic, several authors recently reached the same conclusion. According to them, the concept has been "stretched to cover an ever-wider variety of cases, while the spotlight has shifted from one definitional dimension to another" (Allen et al., 2020, 211). To fully grasp how careers are shaped, and how they may evolve, it is necessary to understand how one gained access to the House before 2017.

Pathways to National Politics

The question of political careers has been widely covered in the social sciences of politics in a long-established tradition (Dogan, 1967). One of these approaches consists in taking into account the last occupation held before full-time political activity. It focuses on so-called *politics facilitating occupations*, the professional activities that are more frequently associated with a later entry into politics (Cairney, 2007). It was in response to this approach that we coded the occupational background of MPs, mentioned above. Another approach, which is also fruitful and widely used, involves categorizing prepolitical careers according to their dynamics. The intuition is that MPs do not progress at the same pace, nor do they follow the same pathways toward national politics. Several channels have been identified, according to the point of departure (local or national) and the pace of the career path (Gaxie, 2000). This second approach is useful when reflecting on the professionalization of politics, because it specifically emphasizes the paths that have led MPs to the House.

This is what we set out to do with my colleagues a previous study (Boelaert et al., 2018). We analyzed the mass of hand-coded data with sequence analysis. Originally used in genetics, the method is now an established part of the social science toolbox. Nowadays, it is used to explore subjects as varied as the analysis of connections between women's work and careers (Aisenberry & Fasang, 2017), artistic careers (Accominotti, 2009), or the analysis of social mobility (Halpin & Chan, 1998). By comparison, the literature on politics is more limited.[8] This probably stems from the fact that the technique was, until recently, relatively unknown in political science. It may also have to do with the stigma associated with descriptive methods in contemporary political science.

Nonetheless, sequence analysis is the most appropriate tool to operationalize concepts like pathways or trajectories, since its goal is to group together individuals with similar careers. It is based on the premise that each individual is represented by a "sequence," a series of events that happen in time. The goal of sequence analysis is to group individuals whose trajectories are similar enough, and to distinguish them from others that are mainly different. In order to do this, the algorithm measures the distance between each sequence, pair by pair. It produces a dissimilarity matrix, on which a clustering is carried out to produce consistent groups.

In this particular instance, the sequences of the MPs were coded according to five possible states. One represents the years spent in a local-level mandate (mayor, municipal councilor, other local mandates). Another represents a national-level position (MP, senator, European MP). A third indicates whether the person had a paid, but not elected, position in politics (this is the case for many staffers). The two other states represent positions outside of politics. The fourth describes situations when future MPs were not in politics whatsoever, and the fifth records the years before the MP's 20th birthday.[9]

There is a specificity to political careers, however. They are structured by the political opportunities that mark the electoral calendar. Typical algorithms for sequence analysis can therefore not be used without difficulty. Here the solution was found in the adaptation, recently proposed by Thomas Collas (2018), based on comparing sequences phase by phase (a phase being an electoral cycle, here every five years). This "multiphase" analysis is better able to take into account structuring moments (elections), because it provides a comparison "sub-sequence by sub-sequence" (electoral cycles). In the present instance, a sequence is defined as a succession of four separate phases, each marked by the previous legislative election—that of 2002, 2007, and 2012. At each one of these dates, the MPs were either in a stable position as an MP, or had very little chance of becoming so during this period.

In a context that is characterized by a clear temporal order, multiphase analysis has an obvious advantage. It preserves the temporal structure in which action occurs, while also allowing us to measure distances between MPs.[10] Another advantage is that it allows us to assign different weights to different sub-sequences in the calculation, that is, to consider a particular long-past event as less important. In this case, the two first phases (up to 2001, and between 2002 and 2006) are given the same weight (1), and then the third and fourth phase were weighted at 1.25 and 1.5 respectively. This comes down to considering that the recent past is more important than the distant past, which we nevertheless keep a trace of. This is a reasonable hypothesis, whether in terms of political careers (the current position provides more direct opportunities than previous ones), and socialization (the current situation is more likely to influence the way someone sees and acts than things that happened over the previous decade).[11]

Figure 2.1 shows a first result of these operations.[12] Each line on the graph represents an individual, each column a year. The color indicates the state, chosen among the list of the five available options. The 11 different groups are the result of the classification produced by the algorithm. For the seven first groups, the individuals were not MPs before 2017. These 410 individuals are, however, very different in terms of their political and professional past, as we can see by their career paths.

Group 1 is made up of those who had no, or very little, paid political occupation prior to 2017. This was the largest numerical group in 2017, with 167 members, and is made up of people who pursued their careers outside politics. Due to substantial differences in age, this career may have been either short or long, as is shown in the gray bars of various lengths. I refer to this group as "civil society," as it is made up of people who were outsiders to the political field before the election, at least on a professional level. Arguably, the term "civil society" is vague; it lumps together different professions, some of which historically have had an easier path into politics (lawyers, doctors, and senior public servants, the so-called politics-facilitating occupations). But it also includes people with a very distinct path to politics, individuals who had never lived "off" politics before 2017. By contrast with previous legislatures, this group is massive. And in the "get-outist" context of 2017, this identity was an important resource that was often highlighted in the campaign.

This is not at all the case of Group 5, which brings together the MPs who were previously political assistants. The green color that dominates in this group indicates the MPs who spent a large part of their careers in politics,

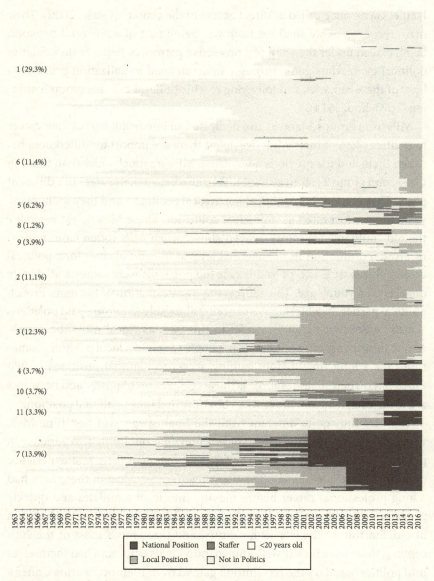

Figure 2.1 Multiphase sequence analysis of careers of MPs elected in 2017.

without being elected. For some, this is the only occupation they have ever had. The individuals in this group are young (42 on average), they may have spent some time in local positions. But what characterizes them best is that they rose to national positions in just a few years, what political scientist

Daniel Gaxie once called a "direct access to the center" (Gaxie, 2000). Their main resource, as we shall see later, was being part of a powerful network, being placed under the wing of a protective patron, or being at the center of political game, thus going through an accelerated socialization process. In light of these remarks, and following recent studies, I call this group "entourage" (Michon, 2014).

MPs from groups 3 (and 8) also dedicated an important part of their career to politics (74% of their adult lives), but there are important differences between them and the previous ones. These MPs are much older than those in the second group 2 (55 on average). They also began their career in a different place. They started their political life in local positions, and they spent many years there, most often as municipal councilor. These MPs might resemble the old "militant" trajectory evoked above, when MPs (often Communist) received a promotion to the national level at the end of their long political career. This is true, except in this case the positions were remunerated early on, even at a young age. This reflects the transformation of the main French political parties, in which activism occurs alongside obtaining paid positions (Lefebvre & Sawicki, 2006). I refer to this path as "local roots" because—unlike the other groups—it points to people who had a local position, sometimes for a long time, before gaining access to national positions—often much later. Their main resource is the accumulation of power and networks at a local level, which in the end can be converted into a national position.

They are thus quite different from the final category of first-time MPs, which brings together those who have a previous, but limited, experience in politics. Groups 2 and 6 share the fact that they had their first experience of politics quite late in life, often after they were 50. Most of these MPs had a long professional career before moving into local mandates and quickly progressing to the national level. This model is reminiscent of the notables of old. Starting in the late 19th century, and throughout most of the 20th century, these were locally well-known individuals who launched themselves into politics based on the recognition gained from their occupations, after a first part of their life dedicated to another profession. Although smaller nowadays due to the rise of other groups, it is still a recognizable model. I call this group the "second career" model, both because this name objectively describes the trajectory of these MPs, and because these MPs often highlight their previous careers when they run for parliament.[13]

In addition to the fact that it quantitatively corroborates classic results about French politics, this typology can also be found, mutatis mutandis, among re-elected MPs. This confirms its stability. Group 11 represents these MPs from civil society (who were fewer in 2012, particularly among those who were re-elected). Groups 4 and 7 include those who spent many years in local positions. Group 10 is a re-elected version of the previously described "entourage" group, those who began their political career young and at the center of politics.

For the sake of clarity, this first classification can be further simplified. Broadly speaking, MPs can be distributed according to two main factors related to their political and professional careers. The first divides the MPs according to the time they spent in politics before reaching the national parliament. In 2017, and indeed before, the length of time spent in politics was highly variable. Some MPs went into politics very young and never left, essentially spending 100% of their adult life in this milieu. At the other end of the spectrum, novices had—by definition—spent 100% of their careers outside politics. However, the second—vertical—dimension differentiates between those who spent most of their time at the local level (municipal council, department, region), and those who spent most at the national level (parliament, MP collaborator, ministerial cabinet etc.). This axis divides MPs who, although they have spent the same amount of time in politics, have worked in completely different conditions. This can be clearly seen in the different types shown in Figure 2.2.

Much can be drawn from this way of representing political careers. The first and most obvious point is that it clearly shows that the term "career politicians" brings together very different types of trajectories and life chances. In this case, sequence analysis helps us to distinguish between two kinds of career paths (local roots and entourage) that are often conflated under this same term. On one hand there are the MPs who had been long

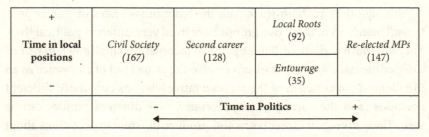

Figure 2.2 Simplified representation of political careers of 2017 MPs (group numbers in parentheses).

involved in their party and were slowly moving toward a national-level mandate, election after election. First involved on the local level, often as municipal or departmental councilors, they were patiently waiting for the party to select them to run for higher positions. Then, if they got lucky, they finally got elected. On the other hand, we find those who entered politics at a young age, most of the time after completing a Bachelor or a Master's degree in a prestigious school. Soon after graduating they were hired as a parliamentary aide or as staffer in a ministerial cabinet, before launching their own career.

These results confirm what many previous studies had already noted, and also offer an empirical, inductive way of investigating political careers. Just as the US amateurs studied by David Canon were not homogeneous, career politicians have taken different pathways that make the group quite heterogeneous. We can see this distinction in the comparison between a low-ranking MP and a presidential candidate like François Fillon. The latter began his political career in 1978, as parliamentary assistant for an MP in the west of France. When that MP suddenly died from a heart attack in December 1980, he quickly found another. Over the course of his subsequent career he has been elected or nominated to all the available positions in politics, be it MP, mayor, minister, county president, region president, and then, finally, prime minister. His career is a clear illustration, and indeed a perpetuation, of the path of rapid ascendancy typical of the "entourage" group. Just a few years after he entered politics, at age 27, he had reached the national level for the first time and he would continue his rise from there. By comparison, his colleagues from the "local roots" group were over 55 years old (on average) by the time they made it to the Lower House. There are dozens of these "local roots" MPs in every legislature, but there is no point naming them because their names will be unfamiliar to readers anyway, given they have been involved in politics all their life but only at lower levels of responsibility.

Although they are both stuck with the ignominious label of "career politician," members of these two groups have lived very different political lives. They also have had very different political incomes—a small-town mayor or a departmental councilor does not receive the same kind of allowance as an MP. Behind the criticism of the representative who has cumulated different positions (and the corresponding revenue), very different profiles can be seen. These divergent career paths also produce different expectations about working in politics—as we will see in the next chapter. They also provide very unequal political opportunities.

Operation Warp Speed

When too much emphasis is put on an opposition between "career politicians" and "others," it can mean these important differences are overlooked. It can also conceal the fact that the key dynamic of 2017 was not the complete renewal of the political class. Rather, it was a massive career acceleration for a good number of aspiring politicians, eager to access higher positions but stuck in the waiting lines. They saved themselves a lot of time waiting when they followed Macron in his successful venture. The analysis should therefore not be limited to the fact that MPs are younger or more inexperienced, as these obvious facts obscure a central trend that sequence analysis clearly brings to the fore: the acceleration of careers for those who entered in 2017.

Sequence analysis reveals this fundamental fact when we use it on the other legislatures. We can see that the overall decrease in time spent in politics before election does not impact MPs in the same way. Arguably, it enabled a large-scale entry of MPs from civil society, and it reduced the overall waiting time. But if we are to look for a winner, the MPs in the "entourage" group are clearly those who benefited most from it. For these MPs, and especially for those affiliated with parties from the majority coalition, the decrease in waiting was substantial. Instead of patiently waiting 13 years like their counterparts of 2012, they now only had to wait 7.5 years before accessing national-level roles. By contrast, MPs from some other groups gained much less time; career acceleration was limited to a select few (Table 2.2).

This twofold difference can be easily explained. Let us take the MPs from the "civil society" group first, and specifically the MPs who had not

Table 2.2 Number of years in politics, by career path

Number of years in paid political positions	6th (1978–1981)	11th (1997–2002)	13th (2007–2012)	14th (2012–2017)	15th (2017–2022)	15th LREM
Civil society	1.7	2	3.7	2.1	0.1	0.1
Second Career	5.6	7.8	7.2	6.9	5.9	5
Local roots	15.6	17.4	19.3	17.5	17.8	16.1
Entourage	9.4	11.6	10.7	13	9.2	7.5
Former MPs	15.9	19.2	22.1	23.4	22	20.1

Before 2017, MPs from the entourage group in LREM spent 7.5 years in politics, compared to 13 years for MPs with the same trajectory in 2012.

been previously involved in a political party. For them, the creation of En Marche! and the call for candidates made an otherwise unimaginable situation conceivable; it opened up the realm of possibilities where it was previously closed. The interviews conducted with these MPs after, often illustrate this. When I first met Martine, she was 65 and had just arrived in the Lower House. She had never even visited it before. She was a retired health worker (in middle management) and had only been elected as an LREM MP for a few days at the time of our conversation. Her political experience was extremely limited. When I asked about it, she mentioned that in 2014, she had been a supporter of a political group that had formed for the local elections in her town, a medium-sized agglomeration in western France. Describing herself as "dissatisfied" with the political offer, she became involved in this "civic movement," which claimed to do politics outside parties. After the election, where none of the group's candidates were elected, she continued to attend meetings for a little time, before her interest waned. This is how she recalls about her involvement with En Marche!:

[In the Fall of 2016], we were talking in this small group. We said to ourselves "that might be a good opportunity" . . . because we're not big enough, it may be a good opportunity to join forces with them [En Marche!] So, the party joined forces with their local committee. And so, we set out to prepare for the presidential elections. And then in our party we asked ourselves, "well, is there anyone who would be interested in trying to be nominated for the upcoming legislative elections?"

Well, it's true that I had thought about it. And I said, why not? It was October 2016. And so, I said to myself, well maybe it's the opportunity to go all the way, because given my age . . . I won't have time afterward. So, there were four of us from this little group to apply. I was the only woman, along with three men. So, we waited for the nominations from En Marche! in January. And then we applied. And so . . . like everyone else, by computer [via Internet]. . . . You know, on the website, then we waited for their decision.

[. . .] Meanwhile, we continued the presidential campaign. One day in April, I was in Paris for the day. And that very day, they called me . . . someone called me from the movement. They wanted to do a phone interview, for 35 minutes, to assess my candidature. So . . . and after they told me, "You must keep this conversation a secret because not everyone will be called." So, I thought well that's a step forward. But it didn't go to my head or anything, I didn't think I would ever get it! So once again, I waited [...] And then, well, it was only on the day when the executive director of En Marche! held the press conference where he announced the list of candidates, that I saw that I had been selected.

Her narrative shows that the En Marche! movement's call for candidates was an opportunity. She submitted her candidature online, and then unlike the other interviewees who were better informed, she simply waited for an answer with no other information, not daring to think it would be positive. She was ultimately nominated, and the three men from her party were not. Martine's candidature is a good reflection of the image promoted by the presidential party; she is one of the people who, although interested in politics, would never have thought about becoming involved at that level.

Other MPs also correspond to this description. Mathieu, for example, was in his 30s, and he had been elected with LREM for almost two years when I interviewed him. A former graduate from Sciences Po, he had then pursued a career in the French administration. When he applied, he was a senior public servant working in a ministry. The process he describes is somewhat similar. He had never been previously involved in politics; he was a regular voter for the Socialist Party but was disappointed by François Hollande's presidency. Yet he had never really considered going into politics himself until mid-2016, when he initially became involved at the local level, organizing support committees for Emmanuel Macron. Then, in January, he too submitted his application online.

But unlike Martine, he had several interactions with "members of the movement," who informed him of the progression of his application. Following their advice, he was even able to modify his choice of constituency after he learned that his initial choice was apparently reserved for another. The logic is the same however; he was typically someone who, under normal circumstances would never have considered becoming directly involved in politics at this level, or even at a lower level. But in this rapidly evolving milieu, he decided himself to join the race. In his own words, he said, "it seemed like at that point in my life I had the opportunity to become an MP, which was quite unexpected, largely due to circumstance, as I explained, and that my role for the future of our country was there, rather than simply being a cog in a wheel [of the administration]."[14]

The logic was quite different for those who were already active in politics. The creation of En Marche! presented them with an opportunity to become involved at a level they would never have dreamed of attaining, and certainly not so fast. For example, the following extract comes from one MP, whom I met in the first months of his first term. He was over 50 years old, and he had previously been a municipal councilor for the Socialist Party in a Parisian suburb for over 20 years.

Why did you decide to run for election?
Well I had already been elected at the local level since 1995 in [Parisian suburb]. Well, it wasn't anything new, it wasn't an entry into politics. Although many of us from civil society have moved in, for some it is an entirely new representative mandate. Others, like myself, have already had a municipal mandate. [...]
Initially I had absolutely no intention of running for the legislative elections. And then in February I said to myself, "well, why not?" "Macron has called on civil society, why not have a go?" It was . . . I wouldn't say it was a spur of the moment decision, but it was not planned from the outset, you know. Me, I've been a representative since 1995 and I didn't have any responsibilities within the Socialist Party, at the federation level or anything else, so I didn't have a clear career plan. I did my work as the principal of a primary school and my municipal mandate alongside that, that suited me fine and then, I had this opportunity, so I took up the adventure.
Ok, so you hadn't even thought about becoming mayor?
Oh, no, no, no. I was a . . . I was just a lieutenant! [laughs].

This narrative clearly reconstructs the chronology of his involvement, which aligns with the chronology of shifting realms of possibilities; from possible, his candidacy became plausible, and then progressively desirable. Clearly the sudden emergence of a party without established candidates gave rise to vocations that would otherwise have remained unexpressed, probably even unimagined, simply because they would have been unthinkable in the previous system. Not anymore. In just a few months, a long-term local representative with no career plan was able to campaign against his own party and win the election. The interview also reveals his interiorization of the norms of the political field, namely the existence of a structured order of succession that governs careers. The "lieutenant," who was once satisfied with his career, decided to launch a campaign to become the commander, when the opportunity arose.

The same logic allowed others, who had had been involved but got tired of waiting, to get back in the race. For some of these MPs of major parties, 2017 was a way of accessing positions of responsibility much more quickly. The interview with a 45-year-old municipal councilor from the small center party MODEM also illustrates this change in career horizons. He had participated in this movement at the national level for several years, first by attending the party summer schools and meetings, and joining its national bodies. But he had gotten worn out and was in the process of removing himself from classic politics when Macron became candidate—with the support of his party:

> A year ago, I didn't even think I would be an MP. In fact, I was seriously thinking of getting out of politics, at least as it is practiced today. I was much more interested in alternative forms of civic engagement. I had followed *Nuit Debout* with interest [a left-wing, anti-elite street movement that took place in 2016 in Paris]. Not that I shared everything ideologically, but the idea of a movement driven by citizens like that, there were interesting things.[15]

But after discussions with other members of his party and when his party's president endorsed Emmanuel Macron's candidacy, he came around. "I said to myself: 'well when it is a historic opportunity, there's a point to being part of the game, to promote certain ideas and push things forward.'" He was then selected to run as a candidate under a party agreement in the June legislative elections, and he was voted in.

Yet for other first-time MPs, the creation of En Marche! above all represented a way of saving time—sometimes many years, in a career that they had already mapped out. This is clearly the case for several of the MPs in the "entourage" group. For these people, the desire to have a career in politics was much more obvious, but they knew they would have to wait for a long time due to the pyramid structure of the profession. There is no shortage of examples of young ambitious people who rose to positions of responsibility in 2017 with a speed that had rarely been seen before. Several former staffers, for instance, became MPs before their 30th birthdays, when others were only slightly older. The MPs in the "entourage" group of LREM were aged 40 on average, compared to 43 on average overall. They had also spent less time overall waiting in holding positions. Even for these individuals, whose careers were already accelerated in comparison to those of their counterparts, their career progressed faster still. For example, one advisor to the former health minister was recruited just as he was finishing his undergraduate degree at Sciences Po. After three years in a ministerial cabinet, he was nominated, at age 28, and subsequently elected. In other circumstances he would have been one of the youngest MPs in the chamber. But not this time, as he was not the only one to benefit from this acceleration. Other cases could be mentioned, and some will be discussed in more depth in the next chapter.

For all of them, 2017 was nothing short of a fast lane into politics. The upheaval of political rules, and the arrival of a party without candidates, created a wide opening that allowed them to move rapidly into positions of responsibility. This change in party affiliation, sometimes quite rapid, should nevertheless not be seen as merely strategic. Among those already involved in politics, those who joined En Marche! probably agreed with the party line it promoted. Whether they hailed from the right of the Socialist Party or from the social wing of some right parties, those who made this partisan migration were often ideologically close to the platform presented by the movement. As political scientist Fabien Escalona noted about them, the shift was not hard to make: "for the tenants of a social-liberal conversion of social-democracy, the Socialist Party was no longer considered as the most appropriate vehicle or medium."[16] In other words, En Marche! served those who were ideologically ready to serve it, but it served them well.

The Moral Economy of the Waiting Line

These opportunities may have been seized without there being overwhelming opportunism, with these newcomers being driven by Bourdieu's "practical sense," a somewhat infra-conscious drive that made them choose and desire what was in their best interest. But this should not obscure the fact that all these MPs benefited immensely from the situation, at least in terms of their careers. They jumped the massive waiting line that had formed in front of them, and by not respecting the established order, they accessed positions of power much more quickly than they ordinarily would have. In so doing, they altered the relatively stable rules for the attribution of positions, in their favor.

The existence of a waiting line implies a series of norms designed to regulate waiting and advancement, and to sanction those who do not respect the rules. These may be more or less explicit rules, but they are generally well-known to participants. And when they are broken, there is always someone to remind the person of what they have done wrong. Several texts in the social sciences have clearly expounded on what we could call the moral economy of the waiting line, this ensemble of norms that organize progress, privileges, and special dispensations, as well as the prohibitions and corresponding sanctions in these specific social forms.

Queues in the USSR have been an object of choice for scholars, due to both the recurrent lack of goods in USSR shops, and to the fascination exerted by the regime. The rules that organized them were complex, invisible, collective, and known to all. A sociologist who studied them at length recounted how, when a queue had formed, a group of people who had probably never seen each other before could "get organized." In just a few minutes, "informal leaders emerged," and if the wait was longer "written lists were drawn up." After a time, "in front of every counter, the crowd progressively became a group" (Coenen-Hunter, 1992, p. 218). Organization allowed them to bring order to a situation of intense competition that might otherwise potentially degenerate. Together, the line ensured that the rules of ordinary priorities would be respected, or at least defended. And if the norms of what was acceptable were flouted, swift calls to order would be issued.

Naturally, this combination of outrage and jealousy came out during the June 2017 elections. Long-time hopefuls who had been patiently waiting their turn were aghast to see the positions they had desperately coveted being snatched up by others in the space of just a few weeks. They protested, sometimes quite publicly. Their frustration, tensions, and altercations were plentiful and relayed by the media. This was not an unprecedented phenomenon. The criticisms were reminiscent of other forms of public recrimination from insiders faced with the arrival of a group of newcomers. In the early 2000s, following a law on gender parity that mandated quotas for women in different electoral bodies, many men had found the career path they envisioned thrown off course as a result. This new regulation disrupted the classic lines of succession within parties, as ordinary compensations in the form of positions were no longer available for these men, who had sometimes been party activists for years. In a matter of a few months, they found that their time investment had lost much of its currency as they were set aside in favor of women candidates, whose involvement was sometimes nonexistent (Achin & Lévêque, 2007). This gave rise to a similar feeling of bitterness and injustice against the recent arrivals.

In 2017, no one was more the focus of criticism about transgressing an established order of politics than Emmanuel Macron himself. By launching and winning this solitary venture, the future president had done nothing more that save himself the incredibly long wait candidates for this position typically face. As we have seen, his profile was only partially atypical for a French politician. In terms of education, his trajectory was typical of the young French elite. Notwithstanding his repeated claims during the campaign, his career more closely resembled that of the MPs in the "entourage" group than those of the "civil society" politicians.

This profile in fact resembles others in the past. During the campaign, Macron was compared to Jean Lecanuet, the leader of the Mouvement des Républicains Populaires which defied de Gaulle in 1965. Lecanuet's rapid rise to power, his modern campaign (he was the first to use television, Macron leveraged "big data"), his centrist position, and even the similarity of the slogans "A new man for France on the march!") were regularly noted in 2017. Macron was also compared to other young groundbreakers, such as Valéry Giscard d'Estaing, the third president of the Fifth Republic, who was the youngest president when he was elected in 1974. Comments about him were also not so far removed from those made about another young political "prodigy," (as journalists called him at the time), Laurent Fabius. The youngest-ever French prime minister (1984–1986), Fabius was also described as being obsessed with speed. His fast-paced career was the object of much discussion and became a defining trait of his media profile. He was described as "a man who loved speed," "a young man of 33 years putting his vast abilities to use for his boundless ambition," a man who was "ready to skip steps" (Sawicki, 1994, p. 46).

But again, although others have been criticized for being too hasty, no one was condemned quite like the new president. On top of the speed of his career, he also skipped a certain number of steps normally considered necessary in the paths to the presidency, for example having been elected locally, being an MP, and even being prime minister—which generally provides both the visibility and the sense of entitlement necessary to run for president. This lack of experience was a common trope during his yearlong campaign. One MP, elected in 2012, said about Macron in 2016: "He is young, talented, and ambitious. I have no doubt that when he is older, with more experience, and has patiently waited his turn, he will be a valuable asset for the Socialist Party, in a few years."[17] But one of the clearest examples of such criticism came from a figure diametrically opposed to that of Macron, former prime minister Jean-Pierre Raffarin. The now senator, who had first entered politics as a political advisor for a cabinet member in 1976 and had had a rich career in various elected positions later, Raffarin embodied *gravitas*—with his slow voice and pace—the typical slowness of those who respect the codes, first among them the order of succession. Interviewed a few days before the presidential election, he once again stressed the importance of the vast experience needed to be head of state. He cautioned the young candidate and called for temperance, essentially encouraging him to "wait his turn," as he himself had done.

> I accuse Emmanuel Macron of being inexperienced. I'm afraid that he will discover certain situations for the first time. The position requires experience [...] *it's too early* for him. *I cannot imagine where he could have acquired the experience* that will give him strength he needs to lead France and stand against Putin, Trump, and the others. [...] I would say to Emmanuel, if I spoke to him so informally, I would say, "well Emmanuel, your time will come, but for the moment it's too soon".[18]

The language is rich with terms that denote the temporal aspect of Macron's progression, and more precisely his all too speedy (in the eyes of his contenders) access to power. A more detailed study of the criticisms leveled at the candidate would show that alongside political accusations, there were just as many criticisms of his political inexperience. In a domain where it is impossible to condemn ambition, probably because it is simply omnipresent, accusations about the transgressions of the norms of progression and the ensuing incompetence were an easier idiom to mobilize.

* * *

Emmanuel Macron's successful irruption onto the national political stage was variously described as a "disruption," a "thunderclap," or a "hold-up." Depending on the political persuasion of the commentators, they either emphasized newness ("a young president," "a new assembly") or continuity ("of parliament of elites," "false novices"). To paint an accurate portrait of the election means trying to reconcile these apparently opposing discourses, at least in part. In 2017 there was clearly a renewal, but only among the upper classes; people who had never had a mandate did gain access to the Lower House, but many of them already had other kinds of political experience. There were a number of true novices who arrived, but also dozens of people who simply accelerated their already established career paths.

To be accurate, one needs to bring together these two aspects of the situation, which both reflect reality in their own way. Less evoked, but no less real was the massive shortcut some took, which led them to skip the long waiting lines to access the political positions. In just a few months, people who had never considered being candidates became MPs, local officials gained access to previously unattainable national-level positions, and young staffers found themselves on the benches of the Lower House. Macron's endeavor opened up a range of possibilities for hundreds of people. The revolution was indeed more than just palace infighting.

The analogy with the waiting line also explains why there were such strong protests against this renewal. What Macron and the candidates from his party did, was not so much simply compete for national positions, it was more that they failed to respect the long-established norms that were accepted by all. What shocked more than anything was the lack of respect for stable rules of career progression. Careers may have been slow or fast, but they were regulated, and contravening these more or less explicit regulations paved the way for accusations of unpreparedness or unbridled ambition. In destabilizing the system of progression in the political sphere, Macron's initiative introduced uncertainty into the organization of careers and endangered work investments that were sometimes decades-long. It also promoted a range of people onto the political stage who were more or less novices. How did they adapt to life in the Lower House? Did they manage to find their place in this highly competitive space and introduce a new way of looking at politics? The following chapter answers these questions by analyzing the parliamentary success of MPs in light of their political backgrounds.

3
UP-AND-COMERS

In the 1939 film *Mr. Smith goes to Washington*, Frank Capra tells the story of the unexpected arrival of a political novice in the US Senate. Appointed following the death of the representative, a local scout leader from Montana, Jefferson Smith, finds himself abruptly thrust onto the national political stage. Capra's camera follows him as he discovers his new milieu. The director portrays him as being moved before the symbols of the nation, worried about the tasks that await him, and enthusiastic at the idea of playing a role in the life of the nation. Capra does not hesitate to mock him too. His repeated gaucheries in this highly codified world are also a narrative trope frequently used by the director.

To the observer of the 2017 legislature, many of the scenes looked eerily familiar. One could even note the differences between experienced MPs and amateurs depicted in Capra's movie. In fact, if one were to zoom out from the scene I described in the opening lines of this book, one would not only see a handful of novices happily wandering through parliament. One would also see other newly elected MPs alongside them, with an altogether different attitude. As I was observing the former in their discovery of the place, I noticed a small group of three 30-something young MPs in a huddle of journalists. Unlike the amateurs I was focusing on, they were not taking selfies or pointing at the century-old ceilings. They were already hard at work. Well aware of the benefit of appearing in the journalists' suddenly depleted address books, they were generously handing out business cards to the masses of reporters present on this first day. As it turned out, this move quickly paid off. I saw these same faces interviewed regularly in the weeks that followed and later, two members of this trio would be offered prominent positions. These were also first-time MPs, but they had solid political experience, as former cabinet staffer or campaign organizers for En Marche! Clearly, they were much more comfortable with national politics than their new colleagues, and they knew what to do on their first day at work.

This scene, with its bumbling novices and its slick and ambitious up-and-comers seems a little too polished to be real. The theme of the "discovery" by new MPs seems like an all too easy angle for a busy commentator, one that would in fact be often used by journalists during the first months of the legislature. And if indeed it existed for a moment, did this gap between the novice MPs and the others last? After these first steps in the National Assembly, is it plausible that the novices successfully adapted to their new work environment, like their colleagues had done before them? To provide an answer to these questions is vital to address the central question of this book, that of the transformative capacity of the amateurs. Did these novices, who were fêted during the campaign for their alleged power to transform the institution and politics in general, actually manage to access positions of power, and change the status quo?

As scholars of parliaments (and of politics in general) know, it is not easy to provide a precise answer to this question. Measuring individual success, or influence, is always complex in contexts where many individuals are constantly interacting. What is more, it raises the question of how success should be measured, given that several important studies on parliaments have demonstrated that there are many ways one can be an MP (Fenno, 2003; Searing, 1994). Using a linear scale to measure success on selected variables, or distinguishing between frontbenchers and backbenchers, does not fully capture the variety of parliamentary roles. Alternatively, one can conduct an in-depth interview a handful of individuals, some novices, some more experienced, to see how they fare. In fact, in the course of my fieldwork, I did use this method to apprehend how MPs differed, how they managed. But regardless of how rich the results provided by this kind of approach were, it would not have offered the more global perspective I needed in order to respond to my question.

Studies on the effects of experience in politics generally face the difficulty of comprehensively estimating practice (and success) in parliament. Not only do such studies require comprehensive and diverse data that is hard to collect, but in order to analyze it they need a method that can do justice to the multiple ways one can be an MP. This chapter proposes a new way around these difficulties, one that leverages the tools and knowledge produced in the currently booming area of computational social sciences. First, it draws on extensive data covering the activities of all the MPs of the 15th legislature, during the first years of their mandate.

For this, I needed access to information that was varied enough to provide an insight into the work of parliamentarians in all its different forms. To collect comprehensive data, I used data that was already available, and I scraped other data from various websites. But I had to supplement this initial data set with other variables, which I deemed important based on my ethnographic work but which did not exist in readily available format. To do so, I compiled other variables, often manually, once again on all MPs. Because it is so consuming and complex, this endeavor is, to my knowledge, the first of its kind—certainly on the French parliament and probably beyond. Yet the main innovation in this chapter concerns not the data but the method. In order to account for the multiple forms of involvement and the various hierarchies that structure the parliamentary space, I had to use a technique that does justice to these patterned, differentiated forms of action. For this purpose, I borrowed a statistical technique from the field of artificial intelligence that does exactly this, an approach called self-organizing maps (SOMs). SOMs are a dimensionality reduction and clustering technique that preserve essential traits of the data set, while making it more tractable.

The result of this analysis is unequivocal. Political novices were relegated to the background of the National Assembly. Members of LREM for the most part, they often remained stuck in subaltern positions, as they were mobilized to carry out the menial and invisible tasks—essentially doing the dirty work. By contrast, more experienced MPs took center stage, sometimes very rapidly. As one might expect, there were some former MPs among them, but also a significant number of first-timers who had previously been employed as staffers. These young up-and-comers were able to immediately activate their knowledge and networks and essentially push in front of more experienced colleagues as soon as they arrived in the House.

These conditions, which are close to those of a natural experiment, allow us to observe the role of previous careers on political opportunities. This chapter therefore pursues the deconstruction of the term "political professional," showing that individuals who come under this label have political "life chances" (*Lebenchansen*) that are radically different from each other. The analysis also demonstrates that the length of time spent in politics is not everything; long-term socialization is worth nothing if it does not occur in the right place, in this case, as close as possible to the center of power. This chapter presents these results and shows the mechanisms through which these differences are produced, and in particular the effect of time on the ways MPs live politics.

Can Parliamentary Success Be Measured?

At first glance it might seem easy to measure the activity of MPs. More than many other groups, and certainly more than any other type of politician, their actions are monitored, recorded, and archived. This abundance of information is, in fact, one of the reasons why so many studies on politics focus on parliaments, despite the fact that their effective power is sometimes limited. The public activities of the houses of parliament have long been reported, in the interests of transparency. Every business day, the *Journal Officiel* (the equivalent to the congressional records in the Anglophone world) publishes information on MPs' activities: the debates of the previous day are fully transcribed, as are results of any recorded votes (most are still held by show of hand). The National Assembly itself produces many records that can be easily consulted. For example, it produces annual analytic tables that summarize parliamentary debates and activities (speeches in the chamber, bills, questions to the government, and reports), as well as tables with information on each MP. These records are in addition to the information summarized in a yearly publication that presents a vast range of other information on parliamentary activities at an aggregate level.

This data (or part of it) is regularly used by the media to scrutinize parliament, to see whether it really is working, and if so, whether it is working more than others have in the past, and who among MPs is the most active. This is not a recent phenomenon. Since the late 1970s, there have been several tables that rank MPs according to their activities, with the results published in the press. These tables present a hierarchy of the "best" and the "worse" MPs in terms of the activities measured. Recently, these rankings have been publicized by the MPs themselves, who post them on their social media profiles—at least when they are good for their image! In other countries, or at the European level, there are similar tables claiming to monitor parliamentary activity.

But these aggregate figures are still a far cry from being an appropriate representation of parliamentary activity. In France, there has been a debate on this subject since an NGO, Regards Citoyens, decided to centralize this information, and even provided its own data, which it had patiently collected using an array of individual indicators (see www.nosdeputes.fr). This data records MPs' presence in commissions, speeches in the chamber, participation in votes, number of amendments voted, and a dozen other pieces of information, almost in real time. Using this readily available information, national and local media have published a number of articles commenting on the level of the activity.

Be they at an aggregate or at an individual level, the analyses produced with these data have been widely criticized. The limitations of a purely quantitative approach to parliamentary activity are well known, particularly when the data is incomplete, or it lumps together indicators that have little in common. What is more, the indicators that are ordinarily used are insufficient to account for the work done by MPs. The number of times someone attended a commission, or the number of amendments they submitted, do not adequately reflect the many facets of their work. Parliamentary work is also collective, shared, and often delegated to one individual on behalf of a group. Likewise, writing a report may take several months, while submitting an amendment may only take a few seconds, so the uncritical aggregation of different kinds of activities therefore does not reflect the actual involvement or activity of MPs. Finally, a whole range of parliamentary activities occur in the constituency and are therefore almost invisible in statistics collected via the National Assembly. Yet the constituency activities, which include representation, meeting with different actors and with citizens, sometimes fill up most of an MP's mandate.

From a research perspective, a final complication is that the publication of these figures has had a practical impact on MPs. This was the reason for a controversy in 2010 between the National Assembly administration and the French NGO Regards Citoyens, mentioned above. According to the former, the group's website was detrimental to parliamentary activity because it encouraged an unproductive inflation in activity. MPs, they said, submitted amendments and spoke in parliament simply to increase their statistics. Although that claim was rejected by the organization, which stated that legislative inflation began before the group was created, it seems that real-time calculation has an impact, both on the type and on the volume of activities in the Assembly. When asked about this, the MPs themselves speak with a rare unanimous voice. Each of them begins by complaining about these rankings "that don't represent their work," and they claim to not pay any attention to them. But when the microphone is turned off, they quickly loosen up. The more reserved among them say they "do what they have to" to not come across too badly on the website's statistics. Others explicitly say they submit amendments or questions simply to stay high up in the rankings. Their aides are even bolder and a few talked openly about—or even showed me—their strategies for improving their positions in rankings.

These strategies are always justified as being necessary. All the MPs interviewed claim that they are often confronted with these rankings and are forced to take them into account. MPs are criticized if they slump in these charts, whether in the local media, in their constituencies, on social networks, or on the national stage. They therefore prefer to adjust their activities rather than face the stigma of a poor ranking, which is interpreted as a sign of laziness. Just like other places where benchmarking has become common practice, Goodhart's law according to which "when a measure becomes a target, it ceases to be a good measure" is clearly relevant in the French Parliament.

The conclusion here is clear. Any attempt to produce a specific measure of MPs' activity seems at best risky, particularly if we limit it to a single composite indicator. In addition to extending the data collection way beyond what is immediately available, we need a measure that reflects the diversity in the range of MPs' involvement on the one hand, and that integrates the fact that MPs do not act in a vacuum, they are constrained by the actions of their peers. But should we manage to do this, a realistic representation of parliamentary activity may be possible. After all, the fact that MPs do not all have the same possibilities to access different positions is part of their everyday lives at the Assembly, and is a factor in the various constraints they are subject, including their political status, and the size of their group. Similarly, the fact that some spend part of their time simply "being present" or "bumping up numbers" and invest very little on the other aspects of the job says a lot about how they use their mandate. Looking at how involved MPs are may be a fruitful avenue for research, on the condition we do not mistake this for an indicator of quality work. In so doing, we are simply looking for a range of different kinds of behavior, and the norms that regulate them, within a given space. This endeavor is quite close to what several scholars describe when they evoke the different parliamentary "roles" endorsed by MPs (Searing, 1994).

With this in mind, I set out to collect data. It is worth pointing out that this phase came after a long period of ethnographic work, which was crucial in understanding what information I needed to acquire, and which sources were reliable. Ultimately three kinds of variables were collected (Table 3.1). The first group combines a series of indicators that allow us to see how legislators contribute to writing the law, how often they participate in what is seen as their core activity. The second type of variable looks at the presence of MPs in the media, both in terms of the volume and the visibility that is received by a given MP. To achieve this, for each MP I collected all

Table 3.1 Types of activities included in the SOM analysis

Legislative activities	Parliamentary reports (number filed); Attendance in Committee (number of attendances); Interventions in Committee (number of words spoken); Interventions in the chamber (number of words spoken); Participation in votes (number); Amendments submitted (number).
Media visibility	Invitations (number): 24/7 news channels; Specialized channels dedicated to parliament (LCP, Public Sénat); National TV and radio, Mentions in national newspapers; Mentions in local newspapers; Number of followers (logarithm).
Other parliamentary activities	Institutional position in parliament (binary); Questions during Question time; Written questions (number, number of ministers); Rooms reserved (number).

the invitations they received to participate in radio or TV shows, mostly via online media programs. I also computed the number of times their name appeared in local and national papers, and to supplement this measure of visibility I downloaded their number of Twitter followers. Finally, a third group of activities was included in order to capture a host of other activities, ranging from written questions to the government, to official functions held in parliament, or simply room reservations. This last group is more eclectic, and some variables may look trivial, such as room reservations. The latter is nonetheless included as a reminder that the parliament is not merely a space for legislating and talking but also a place where MPs construct a political career, and that none of this would be possible or analyzable without capturing the work that goes into organizing meetings and constructing coalitions—all of this being greatly facilitated by the many spaces MPs can reserve in parliament, at the centre of Paris, for free.

Parliaments as Hierarchical, Differentiated Spaces

Capturing the different ways of investing the parliamentary space, and thus the different roles of MPs in all their complexity means taking into account the full range of indicators of activity that we have chosen, in order to observe different configurations. In these circumstances the preferred method is often geometric data analysis. Since it was introduced into sociology in the early 1970s, and then used by Bourdieu to operationalize his concept of field, this statistical method has often been used for the representation of fields and other social spaces (Lebaron & Le Roux, 2013).

There are different subvariants of this geometric method, but whether we use principal components analysis, factor analysis, or multiple correspondence analysis, the intuition is the same. The goal is to reduce the dimensionality of an initial cloud of points (n dimensions) to a more limited dimensional space. This occurs by creating new axes, which are a combination of the initial variables and are chosen based on their ability to minimize the loss of information.

This is not the approach that will be used here. In spite of its well-documented advantages, geometric data analysis presents a number of difficulties for this particular case. Some of these are inherent to the method itself. As the technique reduces the number of dimensions by creating new axes through the *linear* combination of existing variables, it is more useful for identifying overall structures in the data than for smaller, more subtle differences. Minor differences between individuals, which may be extremely significant, are thus hard to see, and even harder to interpret. There are other difficulties relating to the data itself. When the distribution of individuals is deeply asymmetrical (i.e., when certain individuals are very different from the rest), the technique tends to reflect an opposition between these "different" individuals and the rest of the group. The gain in information is therefore limited.[1]

To address these difficulties we can use other, nonlinear, tools to reduce dimensionality, which do not involve the creation of axes through linear combinations of the initial variables. The following paragraphs present one of these algorithms, which may be useful to sociologists, whether for studying parliamentary spaces, or to operationalize a reflection in terms of configurations—whether the concept is field, space, or ecology.

Using Machine Learning to Represent Parliamentary Activity

In order to make this massive amount of data more legible, we used self-organizing maps (SOMs). This algorithm is a type of artificial neural network, the very technique at the core of the current revival of artificial intelligence. Like other neural nets, this approach is not recent. This one was invented in the early 1980s by the Finnish statistician Teuvo Kohonen (1997). Kohonen created SOMs to simplify and to visualize complex data sets, to synthesize the information contained in a multidimensional space. In practice, it brings together MPs with similar profiles into the same spaces on the map and puts MPs with different profiles far apart. Once these calculations have been performed, the algorithm produces a simplified visual representation of the data set, that although flattened onto two dimensions maintains some of the data's essential properties.[2]

By convention, interpretation of this analysis is visual—at least initially. The researcher studies the distribution of individuals and variables in order to determine the "poles" or "zones" of shared practices on the map. Figure 3.1 is a "population map," which presents the distribution of individuals in each of the cells. Some cells contain dozens of individuals, whereas the one in the upper left corner has only six, and its neighbors have no more than a dozen. In this figure we can also see the individuals' gender, indicated by symbols (triangle or circle). In the upper-left quadrant, which we will see is the dominant pole for the National Assembly, there are clearly more men than women.

The traditional approach consists in visualizing the intensity of practices, variable by variable, and then using this information to produce an overall interpretation. Conventional representation of these self-organizing maps is

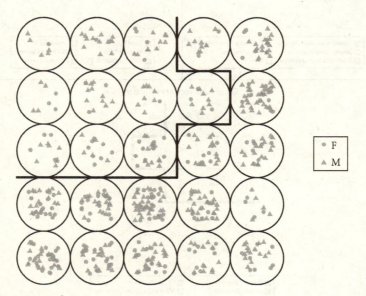

Figure 3.1 Population map.
The map represents the number of individuals per cell.
The exact position of points within the circles is random and should not be interpreted.

88   THE CANDIDATES

therefore a "radar" plot in which each variable is represented by a segment of a circular diagram, of which the length represents average intensity of the practice in each cell (Figure 3.2a–3.2c). The larger this "piece of pie" is, the more frequently the MPs in that cell engage in that activity, on average. On these maps we can see strong variations emerge between actors.

For the sake of clarity, the results are presented by type of activity, but all these maps were calculated using the same data set. The first map reflects the different legislative activities (reports, amendments, presence, and speaking in the chamber). The second shows the different degrees of visibility (media

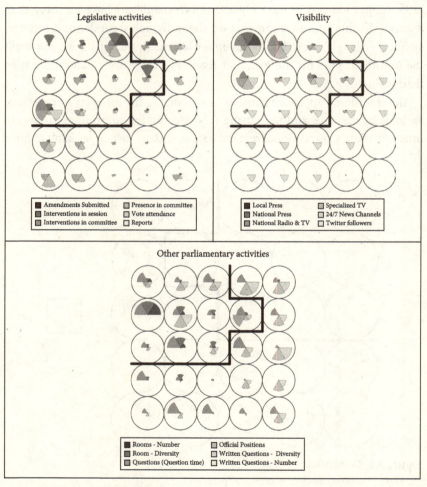

Figure 3.2a–c SOMs of parliamentary practices, radar plot.

invitations, mentions in the press, followers on Twitter). The third describes their involvement in a series of miscellaneous yet potentially important parliamentary activities, since they are indicative of more specific forms of engagement in the Assembly or in the constituency (written questions, room reservations, questions to government, official functions).

The analysis of media appearances is the most straightforward. It clearly shows that a small minority of MPs, situated in the upper left-hand corner, both participate in and are mentioned in the media most often, while those in the lower right-hand corner have little to no media appearances. There is a line between these two points along which media visibility declines. On closer inspection, however, we can notice other variations. The asymmetry between MPs is very pronounced for national newspapers (National Press) and for radio and television at the national level (National Radio & TV). In this space, only a few MPs manage to make themselves heard.

The situation is the same although less polarized for specialized television programs specifically *La Chaîne Parlementaire* and *Public Sénat*, which report on parliamentary activities (Specialized TV). Here we can still see concentrated activity in the upper left quadrant, but it extends beyond this corner of the map. These two channels provide access to a much greater number of MPs, which is a direct result of their purpose, funded by parliamentary institutions as a showcase for the work of MPs and senators. Yet they remain unequal, as most MPs were not invited on these programs at all during the first year of their mandate.

In between the national press and specialized channels there are continuous news channels such as BFM, LCI, CNews, and so forth (24/7 News Channels). This intermediary position can be explained by the programs these channels offer. Most of their time is dedicated to national politics, generally through a debate on a current issue. Essentially organized around debates between political actors, they have greater appetite and are less selective than national channels, which explains this in-between situation.

Finally, the local media provides a slightly different model. On one hand, the MPs in the upper-left quadrant are very often cited. The cell in this corner includes two former candidates to the presidency in 2017 (Marine Le Pen and Jean-Luc Mélenchon), and one former prime minister (Manuel Valls). It is much darker than all the others, even the adjoining ones, which is a sign that national politics dominates coverage of parliamentarians in local media. But there are also gray cells toward the center of the map, which is a sign that certain MPs in these parts of the parliamentary space are also regularly mentioned. The detailed analysis of these results reveals that these are MPs who were for the most part elected during the previous legislature, and who are active in their constituency and are therefore regularly mentioned in the media at that level.

Between the upper-left and lower-right corners there is therefore a continuum between the most visible and least visible MPs, with specificities depending on what kind of invitation they receive. The number of people who follow a given MP's twitter account confirms this logic, with a steady increase along this axis from MPs who do not use Twitter, to presidential candidates with over a million followers each.

Other dividing lines appear on this map. If we look at legislative activities, we can see a distinction between MPs who are actively crafting legislations (on the left of the upper-left/lower-right diagonal), and others who are less so. Some MPs are clearly not very active. They can be seen in the cells on the extreme right of the map, cells which are almost never colored, neither by the presence of votes, by questions to government, or by presence in in committees (even though the difference is smaller here, as repeated absences are sanctioned financially). These MPs are not completely inactive, and in this zone there are also MPs who overinvest in written questions. As we have already mentioned, these written questions are not valued because their impact is considered minor, but they can constitute a signal of interest in the constituency. This strategy is sometimes successful because these MPs may be mentioned in local media, which suggests strong investment to members of their constituency.

Figure 3.3 provides a stylized representation of these results. The National Assembly still appears to be a strongly hierarchical space. The diagonal line running from the upper left-hand to the lower right-hand corner indicates an opposition between very visible MPs and those who remain invisible, whether in the various media or in the Palais Bourbon itself. Party spokespeople, media figures, and former ministers are found in the upper left quadrant. In this respect, the SOM reproduces a fundamental aspect of the institution, the inequality between MPs in accessing rare resources such as the media or frontrunner positions. This fundamental inequality is a typical characteristic of parliaments, one that is demonstrated study after study. Due to the rarity of positions and the concentration of benefits on a minority, certain MPs receive the lion's share.

Other dividing lines structure the space, which is organized in zones reflecting more or less intense practice. The hub of "legislative contributions"

UP-AND-COMERS 91

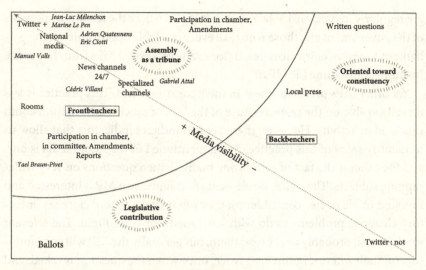

Figure 3.3 Stylized representation of parliamentary activities.

is organized around MPs who participate the most in working on bills and voting on them. If we look at the names of those here, we can see that it is focused on the committee presidents (note, for instance, Braun-Pivet the chair of the Law committee). This is not surprising because chairs are the ones who organize the legislative work in the commissions and then in the chamber. Around them there are majority MPs, with the rapporteurs on texts that demanded long-term work, those responsible for less important texts, and finally many LREM MPs, particularly those who participated in the votes without necessarily contributing to the text.

Other MPs may be very active in the parliament but have a very different kind of parliamentary practice. Those in the upper-left corner, above the diagonal, also participate in the chamber. They also propose extensive amendments; alongside the commission presidents they are the ones who are the most present in committees. This kind of involvement in legislative work should not be confused with that of the majority MPs, and indeed most of those who are in this area of the map are members of the opposition. These are people who are active in the parliament but who have little possibility of seeing their actions translated into legislation. Thus, they use the Assembly as a sounding board, a place where they can gain visibility for their political position via the tools of parliamentary procedure. In this upper-left corner, as mentioned earlier, we can also see former ministers and party leaders who are regularly invited on TV talk shows. It is also where the leading opponents of the government are, those who take every available opportunity in the parliament to make their voices heard (for example, several MPs from La France Insoumise and some LR MPs).

Yet other MPs prefer to invest in their constituencies. This practice is less directly visible on the maps because of the lack of precise information about this kind of activity. However, there are two indirect indicators that allow us to identify signs of this practice. Being mentioned in the local media is one, and the other is the fact of submitting many written questions on very wide-ranging subjects. These may be elements that suggest an MP is interested and invested in his or her constituency, they often evoke school closures or factory closures, problems to do with local roads, or rural flight. The relevant minister will probably never read them, but generally the MP will communicate on their interest in this area twice, once when the question is asked, and then when the response is given. Publicizing questions on social networks is a way of demonstrating their interest in their constituency.

Finally, SOMs can be divided into a series of zones, represented by the solid lines drawn on Figures 3.1 and 3.2 above. This division is produced by an algorithm of classification that combines the cells that are most similar. In this particular case we have chosen a division into two zones that separate high-profile MPs from those with low profiles. The distinction is reminiscent of the one between frontbenchers and backbenchers in classical studies on parliaments in the anglophone world, a division that also exists in other spheres. It should be noted that this SOM operationalizes this division by taking into account not institutional positions, but actual forms of power.

Unequal Life Chances

This map (Figure 3.3) provides a stylized yet highly realistic representation of the first year of the 2017 parliamentary mandate. It also offers a way to answer our initial question about the position of novices in parliament, and more generally about the role of experience in politics.

For this, MPs are positioned on this map based on their political trajectory. The latter was determined in the previous chapter, by a combination of the time spent in paid political positions and the type of position they held. Four of the five previous categories are used as is (*entourage, local roots, second career, former MPs*). The "civil society" category must be refined, however. Although it is useful in responding to questions about professionalization because this group brings together people who have never (or almost never) made a living off politics, it has to be broken down in the context of an analysis of the effects of political experience. The reason is that in this group of people with different profiles, there were first-time MPs who had previously been activists, or had a long experience in politics, but there were also people who were genuinely discovering politics for the first time. This is an important divide between two groups like the France Insoumise (LFI) and La République en Marche (LREM), which combined constitute the majority of MPs in the "civil society" group, but whose profiles differ greatly. Almost all the LFI MPs were already political activists before being elected, while a few dozen of the LREM MPs had never been involved in politics before 2017. To account for this difference, the "civil society" category has been divided into two subcategories: "political experience" and "novices," depending on whether its members were previously involved—but never paid—in politics or not.

How do past political trajectories influence involvement and opportunities for MPs once they are elected? Figure 3.4 shows the distribution of different

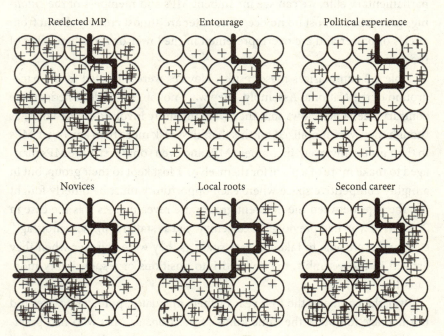

Figure 3.4 Distribution of MPs by type of career in the National Assembly.
Novices were underrepresented in the upper-left quadrant, which represents the frontbenchers.

94 THE CANDIDATES

Table 3.2 Distribution of high- and low-profile MPs depending on their political trajectory

	Frontbenchers	Backbenchers
Local roots	12	88
Novices	13	87
Second career	14.8	85.2
Entourage	25.8	74.2
Political Experience	32.7	67.3
Reelected MPs	36.1	63.9

careers on the same map, this time by type of trajectory. We can clearly see that the political past plays a central role in where MPs are placed—thus in both their role and their capacities for action. Rather than looking at them by cell, we consider their position in two groups, which are already visible on the stylized map (Figure 3.3): frontbench MPs, from the upper-left quadrant, and backbench MPs. Among the first group, which constitutes the parliamentary elite, we can see incumbent MPs and members of the *entourage* group, but almost no novices. The latter are almost entirely absent from circles of power and are overrepresented in the lower or right-hand side of the map.

Table 3.2 summarizes these results. Novices were relegated to the background of the National Assembly. They were not absent or detached; on the contrary, the SOM shows that they were intensely involved in the votes, as though they were mobilized for this thankless task more than any other MPs in their group. Inversely, incumbent MPs and even some first-time MPs managed to make more of a place for themselves. Most kept to their group, but in a highly competitive space where each opportunity must be bitterly fought for, the gaps between the different groups are revealing. As was the case in 2017, MPs who had previously been employed as staffers (in the "entourage" category) were able to take the easy road; as they were younger when they arrived in the assembly, they moved into positions of responsibility more rapidly.

Over the course of the first year of their mandates, political novices did not manage to obtain the same kinds of positions as MPs who had previously been involved in politics. What was true in previous decades remained unchanged with the 2017 election, even though the latter created upheaval in the political field. In reality, the internal hierarchies within this world were not radically changed. The inequalities that existed long before this date essentially remained the same. Even more remarkable is that this remark holds true for other groups. The hastiness of the MPs in the "entourage" cluster, this celeritas specific to these young up-and-comers, contrasted with the gravitas of the two other groups that were previously active in politics ("local roots" and "second career") which are characterized by their lower success rates. The difference between the groups is clear and leaves little room for doubt. In effect, not much had changed in the brand new parliament elected in June 2017.

One possible objection might be that these results, based on the first year, do not allow for the fact that novices may have developed these skills over time, after a difficult beginning. To verify that this was not the case, I conducted a similar analysis for the third year of the mandate (between August 2019 and August 2020). The same variables were collected, and the same analysis conducted as for the first year. The conclusion, mutatis mutandis, is that the same differences can be seen between the groups. Novices were no more successful in forging a path to central political positions in their third year. The time spent—in politics or any other activity—prior to election is clearly crucial (Bresson & Ollion, 2022). Other elements also point in this direction. In a recent analysis of MPs' online communication, Mathis Sansu showed that these groups differed significantly during their term (Sansu, 2022). Using state of the art text analysis techniques, he showed that novice MPs tweeted less, less about national politics, and also less negatively than their entourage colleagues—the latter showing the same patterns as reelected MPs. This was true during the first year, but also in the ensuing four years, although to a lesser extent. The learning process, if it happened, did not conceal the differences between MPs.

Another possible objection is that another variable, quite independent from political experience, is involved. To test this hypothesis, I conducted a further series of analyses. In particular, I ran parametric regressions in order to determine the role of experience in parliamentary success. The results all point in a similar direction. All things being equal, the effect of political experience, whether it is time spent in politics or previous occupation as a staffer, is visible irrespective of the political party. Not all coefficients are significative to the 5% threshold. This has to do with the overall small number of individuals used to compute the regression. It also has to do with the overlap of several characteristics in addition to that of being a novice. Upon closer inspection, it appears that novices were most often young, female, and with lower qualifications than the average MPs for LREM. This, in turns, reveals a strategy used by LREM executives as they recruited candidates. They concentrated all signs of "diversity" onto these novices. Put otherwise, they had the novices bear the brunt of the social representativity they so often claimed during the campaign. Further research should refine this analysis, but for now it seems clear that past experience in politics played a central role in the political life chances of MPs.

The Passing of Time

Knowledge and Acquaintances

One aspect that is often overlooked in debates on the professionalization of politics is that the time spent in politics is also time spent training future MPs. Although it is quite rare when dealing with politicians, another definition of professionalism in virtually all other occupational areas emphasizes skills, what was acquired during the years spent learning the craft. But despite being quite obvious, this is a trait that is rarely mentioned when talking about politicians. Indeed it is unusual for MPs to attract attention to their political experience—especially in times like 2017, when the campaign was particularly focused on newness and fresh faces. However, the effects of this experience became abundantly clear in the first weeks of the new parliamentary season.

The most obvious illustration of this is the little blunders that the new MPs made—most often novices, but sometimes former local council members as well. Parliamentary journalists, more seasoned MPs, and opposition members took every opportunity to make fun of the awkwardness of the newcomers. Of course, in such a highly codified space, mistakes are easy to make. I remember my own difficulties in my first weeks of fieldwork, when I struggled to understand the intricacies of parliamentary procedure. Learning it felt like studying law again, with its arid and procedural approach. But knowing the rules in the National Assembly is key to effectively intervening in the sessions. If used wisely, the small tricolor book that defines the procedures provides the keys to greater power, whether by gleaning precious minutes of speaking time by calling a point of order, or whether by accelerating a vote, or bringing down hastily written amendments.

As could be expected, novices did not know any of this, and their hesitations did not go unnoticed. From their first days, several media outlets relayed the difficulties new MPs faced in the House. Humorous or accusatory, the tone of these articles about the blunders of the new MPs peppered the news in the months after the elections. One was laughed at for forgetting to turn off her microphone, just when she was complaining about her colleague's apathy; another broke down in embarrassment when it came to asking a question of the government. Another, who was supposed to be presiding over a session, found herself entirely in the hands of a parliament official who talked her through everything she had to say and do. The camera mercilessly showed her repeating, word for word, what the public servant whispered in her ear for several long minutes.

One of the sessions I attended was particularly chaotic. It took place on an evening in July 2017. The president of the session was a first-time MP. She was not even a novice; she had previously been a municipal councilor in a small town for over a decade, but it was a part-time job, and the scenery was certainly less intimidating. Right after her election, she had been appointed vice president of the Assembly as part of the approach to renew people in key roles. This is what I wrote in my field journal following this session:

> While not exactly a novice, the session president this evening did not have experience in the Assembly, nor of the running of a session. She did not grant speaking rights to MPs who requested them, even though they have a right to speak. This led to anger among veteran MPs. One member of the majority, asked her, "Madam, excuse me, you signaled to me that you would allow me to speak, why have you not done so?" The president murmured in response, "Because . . . because we have already heard two speeches on this point . . . ." Procedurally, this argument is not valid, and did not satisfy the more experienced MP, who got angry and—in spite of his microphone being switched off—continued, "You may be the Vice-President but I am an MP like you . . . !" And as the conversation was continuing without him, he ostentatiously left the chamber. [. . .]
>
> The ordeal was not over for the session president. She later got lost in the procedure and was having the amendments examined in an unconventional order. Generally, the main amendment is examined first and then, if it is rejected, the "fall back" amendments are examined. But the session

president was doing the opposite, and criticism abounded. "Waste of time!" some yelled, "Completely confusing," complained another. Accusations of manipulation were voiced: was this unlikely order chosen in order to allow a second vote on an amendment that had been pushed back because the majority MPs—some of them novices—had ... forgotten to raise their hands?

Chaos ensued, and the president lost her footing. Despite the best effort of the parliamentary officials, now fully dedicated to helping her out, order was not restored. A right-wing MP, also experienced, seized this opportunity to drive the point home. Visibly annoyed, he addressed the Assembly during a call for order, declaring in front of everyone: "Listen, the learning period is over! The principle is that the main amendment is studied first, and then the secondary amendments." He concluded tersely, "We make the law here, so the regulations must be followed."[3]

In the early months, this kind of episode would be repeated several times. From the perspective of the officials responsible for helping MPs with their work they were more frequent than usual. But a year later most of these new MPs had learned the ropes and adapted to parliamentary work. Like their predecessors before them, they had gotten used to the routines, at least enough to navigate them without too much difficulty. The "blunders" of these new MPs were no longer a part of the daily discussions among journalists who had previously been so hungry for them.

But these were not the only kinds of knowledge needed, far from it. Because of the limited number of opportunities and large number of candidates, it is difficult for MPs to obtain a mission, or to effectively intervene in the space awarded to them. Knowing how the Assembly functions is absolutely crucial. For the most part, this means having a good knowledge of the positions that are coming up for renewal within the Assembly. More generally it is important to obtain information before others, to be able to assert oneself, and not hesitate to take the initiative. Novices are not the only one who need to learn. One socialist MP, whom I met during the previous legislature, discussed this gap between established MPs and new arrivals—even if the latter had had a long local career in politics (like himself):

So that [parliament] was a major discovery for me, especially in comparison to all the MPs who had been staffers, or who worked as aides to a cabinet member before their election. It's true that I had already been invited to Parliament before I was elected, but I was always in the wings [. . .] So [lacking this knowledge] that was a real handicap, a genuine handicap, because it's also a kind of learning . . . a real learning curve that makes me think that today [four years after his election] I'm more of an extra than a real actor. I want to be an actor, but to be one, you have to know the roles and how to play them.[4]

The interview underlines what we also see in the statistics, that among the first-time MPs, some are better equipped than others to assert themselves rapidly. It also shows that some of what makes MPs efficient cannot be learned quickly. Four years after being elected, this MP still regretted the fact that he had not managed to assert himself and hoped to do better in the next legislature. He did not get that chance, however; he was beaten in the 2017 election.

Years spent in politics are therefore above all used to acquire knowledge, especially if this knowledge is acquired in the right places—in this instance as close as possible to the heart of national politics. This time spent close to front-ranking MPs is useful because it is an important way of gaining an understanding of how these institutions function. We can see this in the case of one young MP, Aurélie. Although she was a first-time MP, politics was not new to her. Then in her early 30s, she had been active in left-wing politics since she was 15 years old, later joining the Socialist Party, where she was an active member. She was elected as a municipal councilor in 2014 on the Socialist ballot, before she changed affiliation and was elected as an LREM MP in 2017. She was thus not unfamiliar with the inner workings of politics, but because she came from outside Paris and had not gone through the ministerial cabinets, she was not part of what she described as the "little group of a dozen people who gravitate around the Elysée Palace" (the seat of the presidency). Despite this, she knew where to look and who to contact to make herself heard:

> Well I have a tiny example, I don't know if you saw it, *Le Monde* [the elite's newspaper] ran a story last weekend on my member's bill [. . .]. But you can't imagine how hard I fought for it! So, it's not a legislative proposal, because an MP cannot propose a law that creates an additional administrative strata [. . .] But I tried hard to make it happen. I had meetings, I called Matignon [the prime minister's office], the Elysée [the president's office], the minister of justice's cabinet, and then spoke with [the French ombudsman], to stack all the odds in my favor.[5]

Prior knowledge, acquired during the long years of waiting to become an MP, are crucial to a parliamentary career. Especially, as was the case for Aurélie, when they are associated with the creation of a network. That is exactly what Aurélie was able to mobilize to defend her bill. Her former mentor, a senior Socialist Party figure in her region, had been appointed a minister and had taken her under his wing. He had invited her to events at the ministry, where she was able to meet key cabinet members, and other officials, who informed her on what to do, and when.

This is an important difference. Some MPs have the knowledge, they possess the codes, but they do not have acquaintances that will help them. Mathieu, also mentioned in the previous chapter, is a case in point. A former senior public servant, he knew the functioning of the Assembly and they administration better than many MPs. He also rapidly understood that command of parliamentary process was precious. As a novice, as soon as he took office, he hired an experienced parliamentary collaborator to guide him through the intricacies of the Palais Bourbon. He had been warned that the first weeks would be decisive, he positioned himself strategically. He obtained the committee he wanted, and rapidly obtained additional responsibilities. This is how he described his first months at the Assembly:

> At the beginning, there were not many members of the committee who were familiar with the important reports, the ones that matter. And so, to a certain degree, if you were well-informed like I was, you could have a relative advantage, which was important. From that perspective, the beginning of my mandate was quite positive.[6]

Yet when I met him in April 2019, he was disappointed. He said that he had struggled to successfully do what he had set out to do, and that this "positive beginning" had not been followed by concrete results. He found that what he considered his skills, composed of technical knowledge and a sense of politics acquired in administration, were not valued. "Making a space for oneself among 310 peers is complicated" particularly given that he considered the "management of human resources" defective. On one hand, he criticized the group for not encouraging people (like himself) who had specific skills, but trying to please everyone. According to him, the Commission president spent his time "handing out distinctions, because it's not really much more than that, not because of their skills, but just to keep people busy."

Above all, he was frustrated to see some of his colleagues, who were also first-time MPs but who were former political aides, snatch up positions of power. He described these figures in rather ungracious terms, a sign of his frustration at having his participation restricted. According to him, this minority successfully managed to hoard all the key missions and roles, even the minor ones, without any thought of accommodating others. The difference between him and them was not skills, but contacts.

The responsibilities he obtained in the parliamentary committee, which he initially saw in a positive hopeful light, did not bring about the desired results. Even in his constituency, where he would have liked to gain a foothold and run for mayor, he could not find an opening. When I asked him about it, he did not think he would run for election in the town that he represented as an MP, "it would be very unlikely that that door opens for me, probably only a 5% chance, because there are people who were positioned very early on because they were involved, they were already established in the political scene." And when we talked about his re-election, in a context where the executive was considering reducing the number of parliamentarians, he concluded bitterly "so there will be no longer a place for people like me, in 2022. And I think that you can check, in many regions, there will be no longer be a place for people who came up, like me, in 2017 and who don't have role in the system."[7]

Waiting and Expectations

Skills and networks are thus central to success, and former political aides who arrived in 2017 had had time to accumulate them. The long hours spent conducting fieldwork, interviewing, and observing MPs leads us to envisage an additional, complementary, explanation for their success. This one is based on the impact that waiting has on the feeling of legitimacy in this sphere. As we have seen, although novices did not always have the knowledge or skills required, some of them had a clear sense of ambition. This was Mathieu's case. He was determined to make a space for himself, he was organized and prepared, and yet, by his own admission, he found himself marginalized because he was not in the right networks. But the new arrivals were not all as driven as Mathieu. Many were much slower, or just intimidated. Another factor that seemed to come into play was that having waited for too long led to a self-effacement among certain MPs. Conversely, others who had progressed more quickly—in politics, or in their career overall—had a sense of self-confidence that facilitated their success. In other words, having gone through a long period of waiting disciplines individuals, it imposes on them a sense of limits, while having skipped the wait was more often associated with sense of entitlement that, in turn, favored success.

This question of attitudes toward time has been studied extensively in sociology. In one pioneering study on how the passing of time had an impact on individuals, *Marienthal, the Sociography of an Unemployed Community*, sociologist Marie Jahoda and her colleagues showed that increasing unemployment had altered the collective and individual life rhythms of the inhabitants of this small town. As their hopes of finding work faded, these unemployed workers changed their behavior and their attitudes toward time (Jahoda et al., 2017 [1993]). Their demands in terms of salary, working conditions, but also their lifestyles and hopes for the future all declined. Another example comes from Javier Auyero, who studied the waiting period imposed on members of the working class in accessing social services in Buenos Aires, and showed how this wait was used as a tool to dampen any kind of protest among vulnerable communities. In *Patients of the State* (2012), Auyero shows how this perpetual position as an applicant, waiting to receive benefits, fosters an anxious attitude toward the future that is neither conducive to collective action, nor indeed to any type of action—for fear of retaliation. Moreover, those who have been dependent on welfare for a long period of time have internalized their position as dominated subjects, they have been disciplined by the wait.

Yet the unemployed, or members of the working class, are not the only ones who feel the effects of this kind of waiting. The same kind of dynamics are at play for the MPs. They clearly construct an opposition between MPs who have waited patiently for years, and those who have not waited at all. The first-time MP mentioned above, who wanted to become an "actor" rather than being simply an "extra," is a good example of this. He was used to having to wait in his local mandates and continued to do so once he was in the Assembly. But other new MPs had no intention of waiting. In the introduction to this chapter, we saw how certain first-time MPs had begun to liaise with journalists from the very first day of their mandate. Among them, my attention was drawn to one in particular, a former aide to a prominent politician. Here is what I wrote in my field journal that day:

> Generally speaking, there are MPs who wear their badges and those who do not. Those who have been re-elected don't wear them. But a few among the

newcomers aren't wearing them either. They also seem more self-assured. [...]

The attitude of [this MP] illustrates this well. He looks quite different from the others. He seems very comfortable here [in the parliament], moves rapidly through the corridors, and gives the appearance of being very familiar with the environment, like many who have been elected before. In the chamber, where the official photos are being taken, he skirts the queue that his peers form to go talk to the photographer (but doesn't have his photo taken). He does not show the excessive politeness other MPs display on this first day. He does not greet the officials as he walks pass them, does not look at the MPs.

Everyone clearly knows who he is, and he knows it. The difference between him and some of the others is remarkable. The latter are often uncomfortable, some of them even asked me if I could take a photo of them, or even if they are allowed to take photos.

In the five minutes he spent in the *Hémicycle*, he even climbed up onto the speaker's platform (nobody had dared to do this in the time I was observing), looked authoritatively out over the chamber, and then rapidly came down, and left.[8]

Over the course of the first year of field work, the same scenes would be repeated, over and over. Former staffers and former members of ministerial cabinets always gave the impression they were two steps ahead of the others. The fact that they knew how the mechanics of parliament worked, and knew those in positions of authority, was clearly essential; but it probably was not sufficient on its own. There was something in their attitude to time that made them go faster. Something that perhaps could be described as a sense of entitlement, which makes individuals dare, take risks. In an environment that is competitive and favors initiative, this attitude can be highly profitable. Once again, there is a sociological explanation for what might otherwise seem like a psychological trait. It might seem that people who rose rapidly in their careers, who always went faster than others, did not have the self-discipline of those who waited. But it also meant that they tended to consider everything within their grasp. Unlike those who waited, these up-and-comers have a strong belief in their ability to rapidly fulfill their objectives, having never yet been proven wrong.

Novices provide a perfect case study of these different relations to time and their effects on self-assurance. Within this group of novices, some had waited and others not. We already met Martine in Chapter 3. A former nurse who became a manager in a hospital later in her career, she was one of the MPs I met with several times in the first years, to document her integration into parliament. From the very first weeks of her mandate, she herself noted that certain members of her group had "different levels of ambition." In our first interviews, she told me that some "wanted to assert themselves quickly," that they "wanted to table amendments quickly," or that they "volunteered to become rapporteurs." One year later, I asked her to comment again on these contrasting attitudes, to see if they were still relevant:

> **It's already been a year since the election, how do you feel? What is your dominant feeling?**
> Well the dominant feeling is progressive settling in, I would say.
> Ok . . .
> Compared to what I had set myself, as a goal, to move forward one step at a time.[9]

This "step by step" integration, as she put it later in the interview, was clearly different from that of MPs who took on responsibilities—sometimes at the expense of their colleagues. Among the more ambitious group there were many former staffers, but also a few novices. This was the case for Laurent, for example, who had previously been human resources director in a major company, with a spectacular career trajectory. In just a few years he had gone from being the manager of a shop, to managing company-wide policy. He explained to my colleague Juliette Bresson, who interviewed him repeatedly as part of her dissertation, that when he arrived in parliament he had not been interested in waiting.

> Everyone is an actor. If you're a new MP and you go into a formidable machine like the National Assembly, and you say to yourself [his voice changes, turns nasal, to imitate foolishness] "Oh, I'll see, they'll think of me eventually," that is not going to work. You know, in business, in life, anywhere, you can wait forever before they think of you! That isn't exactly how it works [. . .] It's not like lotto: there weren't 313 little balls and then my number came up. I could wait and say, you know it's not my turn, but it's not like lotto! There's not like 313 balls and then my number!
> **So what did you do?**
> Well, I had to go and make things happen. I had to get information, I had to fight, I had to debate. Well, I say I had to fight, it was all very friendly, don't worry! But you have to explain, you have to say why you're interested,

you have to write, you have to call, you have to try and see people. Obviously if you just sit in your office and wait for the phone to ring, you can wait for Emmanuel Macron to call you but, I doubt that will happen! Right? Because, me, he didn't call me, you know, I promise you, he didn't call! But he didn't call me any more or less than those who complain "oh but people don't know me" [he mimics a whiny voice].[10]

It is well-worth citing this excerpt at length, because the interviewee clearly reveals the lack of understanding that certain MPs who managed to make a space for themselves express with regard to others who, according to them, lack motivation and drive. This interview shows that, unlike other MPs, Laurent did not have the impression that he had to wait patiently before trying to access positions of responsibility. He took every available opportunity—and he also created them.

What is behind these differentiated attitudes toward time? Gender is an obvious candidate. Numerous studies have shown that women tend to be less assertive in the workplace than men, an attitude that hampers their chances for promotion. In a preceding chapter, we saw that Martine had long hesitated to present her candidacy, and that she did so only because En Marche! made it possible to do so online, thus preserving her anonymity, and at the same time preserving her from the disparaging comments from her entourage. Just as political ambition is clearly not interpreted in the same way for men and for women, there may also be a gendered response to waiting, where women would be encouraged to be less entrepreneurial in order to avoid being called out. This would, in fact, be a fruitful avenue for future research.

But there is probably another factor, which is related to the speed at which individuals progress. We could hypothesize that one of the differences between Martine and Laurent, who were both novices and who both had upwardly mobile careers before being elected, is the speed of their progression. One climbed the echelons step by step and finished her career as middle manager, while the other, 15 years her junior—climbed the company hierarchy in just a few years and became an important leader. Never having been faced with long phases of waiting, he could not understand this patience, which he saw as a lack of drive among his colleagues. Having never really experienced failure in his own trajectory, and having been successful in his past initiatives made him cultivate a belief in personal abilities, rather than in the norms that shape the sense of entitlement.

* * *

In *Mr. Smith goes to Washington*, morality ends up prevailing. When the shady governor explained to his acolytes, who were as anxious as he was to preserve their influence in Washington, why he had chosen Smith, a total novice, he said he had found "a perfect man. Never in politics his life, [he] wouldn't know what this is about in two years, let alone two months." The governor concluded, "and the important thing, and this was the genius of the stroke, it means votes!" They were proven wrong. After a series of twists and turns, Jefferson Smith manages to pass the bill he was promoting and expose the corruption that reigned in Washington.

Fiction sometimes trumps reality. The novices elected after Emmanuel Macron's victory did not pass much legislation, nor did they threaten the established order. Having been an effective electoral sales strategy during the campaign, they then became an important source of support for the government. Aside from minor oppositions and a handful of nonconsequential departures, they held firm behind the president. On an everyday level, they assiduously participated in the votes, more than their fair share. In what looks like a cunning of the executive reason, those elected to transform the system from the inside gave the government a solid majority that allowed Macron to govern with little concern for the legislative branch, thus allowing the president to practice politics in the most traditional fashion. As disappointing as it is for those who believed in the transformative power of novices, whether in government or in civic movements, this example shows that a change in casting is likely to not be sufficient to deeply reform politics. I shall return to this in the conclusion. The next chapter looks more closely at the new MPs' surprises, and their discovery of this unexpected milieu. Through this, it expounds some of the more salient aspects of the contemporary political condition.

4
LIFE CHANGES

"These are people who had their lives changed overnight.... They have been thrown in the deep end, like in a pool, and they'll only get out in five years."[1] This comment, made by a journalist familiar with the parliament, is a good summary of what many MPs experienced during their first months in office: a radical life change. Others confirmed it in more positive terms, "it's like entering a washing machine," "it's tough," or again, "I gained weight and I lost friends." These remarks came from first-time MPs who joined the ranks of the Lower House, and took on positions they had only previously seen from a distance. But these complaints were especially frequent in the interviews I had with the political novices who entered politics when they entered the Palais Bourbon in 2017. One first time MP interviewed by Juliette Bresson even confessed that she would sometimes cry on Sunday evenings, for fear of the week to come (2018).

This chapter takes this incursion of novices into national politics as a starting point. How did they adjust to their new life? Did they experience a major change, and is that how they perceived it? And what is it that they found surprising, difficult, or pleasant? Following on from the previous chapter, which reflected on the causes of the limited success of the amateurs, understanding the lived experience of these citizens-cum-politicians can shed light on the reasons that they failed to make a place for themselves among the key actors in the Assembly.

In so doing, the chapter builds on a long line of recent studies looking at these new arrivals in politics. Early on, James Q. Wilson analyzed the difference between amateurs and politicians in Washington, thus offering one of the first long depictions of what differentiates them (Wilson, 1962). David Canon's book later refined this analysis, in particular by showing that this group experienced their new life in different ways depending on a series of variables (1990). Several studies focusing on late arrivals in the political game, women in particular, also showed the specific roles they could endorse while they detailed the mechanisms of relegation (see for instance Achin, 2016). The same is true in France. Several studies have cogently explored the difficult initiation of new arrivals in various moments in time. To cite just two, Michel Offerlé studied the workers elected to municipal councils in the 1880s (Offerlé, 1984), and Annie Collovald investigated the arrival of amateurs in the wake of the French Poujadist movement in the 1950s (Collovald, 1989). Both scholars showed that these newcomers' approach to politics, their ways of speaking, and their expectations of the institution were all off the mark in this highly codified milieu. They also noted that contrary to the image of the naive novice, these new MPs could not help but be aware of the fact they were out of step, which often led to their voluntary self-effacement. Other studies could be cited to document this learning curve, or the more or less long-term strategies for adapting to a political career.[2]

While this chapter builds on these works, the goal here is slightly different. It focuses on these novices in order to use them as a lens to investigate some of the most salient traits of national politics in the early 21st century. Just like objects plunged into a liquid reveal the forces they are subjected to, novices constitute a prime site for observing the pressures politicians are faced with. My intuition was that by asking them about their "surprises," their "frustrations," their "joys," or their "unease," the new arrivals would reveal some of the salient traits of the contemporary political field; that they would offer a synoptic perspective on the "pool" into which these MPs are thrown, to use the terms of the journalist quoted above.

In other words, my goal is no so much to describe a particular aspect of political life as it is to dissect the *modern political condition*, this shared social and material framework in which politicians, both men and women, live and work.[3] By doing so, I attempt to apply a precept once formulated by Loïc Wacquant. Writing about boxers, he lamented that sociology all too often restricts itself when it considers its subjects as disembodied objects, rather than what they are, bodily beings of flesh and blood, emotions, and beliefs (Wacquant, 2015). The same is true of those who engage in politics. Politics is a greedy, all-encompassing activity, which involves bodies and emotions as much as the calculating spirit to which parliamentary action is often reduced.

Interviews and observation reveal the texture of everyday experience. They tell a story where time is dilated, where hectic rhythms are followed by long periods of constrained waiting. They demonstrate that politicians have to deal with very real everyday publicity, which is sometimes unwanted, and where their anonymity as ordinary citizens is a thing of the past. They also illustrate the violence of politics, an activity where blows are regularly traded—metaphorically or not—and where tension is pervasive.[4]

Considered together, interviews and observation outline important elements of this specific world that laypeople have broken into and were asked to adjust to. Most did not, or not entirely. Here too, having waited in the long line that led to national positions, that is having been socialized into politics meant former staffers were better adjusted to the new milieu. And while novices were not able to "change lives," as many had hoped before they arrived in parliament, they clearly had to change their own lives.

A Dilated Time

What is the time of politics? This apparently trivial question has no obvious answer. To just consider that it is hectic, like observers often do, or to say that it is trapped between the long term and the immediate present overlooks important aspects of the question. Political sociologists have investigated the different dimensions of political time extensively, the rhythm of politicians' lives in particular. Using their diaries or using interviews, researchers have studied attitudes toward time in this milieu. The conclusion most commonly drawn is that, in politics, the pace is frenetic. This is what Rémi Lefebvre's study of MPs who cumulate different political mandates in France powerfully demonstrates. For these MPs, for whom politics is more than a full-time activity, the tempo is "relentless," the rhythm is "extremely intense, a constant and compulsive race against the clock." And Lefebvre continues, "politics is a life of excesses, of stresses, meetings, demands, meals, and travels" (Lefebvre, 2014, pp. 124).

The novices I spoke to in the Assembly confirm these remarks. One first-time MP confirmed, "we have weeks where we're sitting from Monday at 4 pm, sometimes right up to Saturday or Sunday, when we start at 9:30 am and finish at 1 am in the morning! It's, I don't know, 12 or 13 hours per day. . . . You've no time to do anything else, it makes you go a bit stir crazy."[5] A recent study based on around a hundred interviews with MPs confirms this. Depending on the week, political group, or other personal factors, MPs work anywhere between 50 and 100 hours—spread between their obligations to be present in Paris, and time spent in the constituency.[6]

Mathieu, the former senior civil servant mentioned in previous chapters, provided a point of comparison with another activity also known for being immensely time-consuming—being an aide in a ministerial cabinet. He emphasized that the number of hours is not everything. As well as the sheer volume, it is the pervasiveness of politics that is difficult to manage; it works its way into all aspects of life, without any clear limitations.

> It takes all your time, something like 80 hours a week. It's not all equally intense, so I wouldn't say it's an impossible job. . . . I've been in much more difficult jobs in terms of intensity and pressure in the senior civil service. Because when the minister asks you to write a memo at 11:00 at night he wants it on his desk at 8:00 in the morning, he's the minister and you don't want to mess around. Here, you have some latitude, because you're the boss. As an MP, of course, you have to deliver, but still . . . . You can organize your time, and so on. But you never get away from politics. . . . Maybe a little on Sundays, for a few hours, with your partner, or whoever, but you'll still have messages, little things. . . . It's really very complicated to get away.[7]

Another novice also mentioned the all-encompassing nature of political activities, describing how the role had taken over everything a year after she began: "It is constant work, you're always busy with a multitude of things [. . .] It is difficult to learn to manage personal life, and professional life, and to combine the two."[8]

Sociologist Muriel Darmon has shown how, in the context of the classes preparing to competitive exams (clearly different but equally constrained), time shortages have significant consequences. One of these is the feeling of being perpetually overwhelmed. The same quickly happened in parliament. Complaints expressed by new MPs cited in the media only six months after their arrival all reflected this difficulty. Some novices even complained that they were suffering from burnout. Adjusting to the frenetic parliamentary rhythm, they said, was difficult. Far from being staged or a simple discourse geared toward the media, this complaint comes back incessantly in my interviews. A former high-school teacher, the president of a permanent committee readily mentioned how this parliamentary rhythm left an impact on his everyday life. During a lunch with his staff after the Christmas break in 2017, he told them how he had become stuck in the parliamentary tempo: "I did basically nothing for four days, I didn't work at all, but in spite of that I spent all my time standing up [laughs]! My wife kept saying, 'come sit on the beach,' but I couldn't stop. I cleaned the beach; I cleaned the terrace. . . . I couldn't just do nothing."[9]

The impact of this rhythm on personal life was significant too. During the first winter, journalists began to mention the possibility of a wave of divorces among novice MPs. Ultimately it didn't happen, but tensions were clear in relationships that were not used to this constant temporal (dis)organization. Less than a year into his first mandate, Mathieu said in a disillusioned tone:

> **So, how have you progressively managed to combine your private and professional lives?**
> Well, let's say that you have to make the choice to give up personal life, family life, and friends. That's it. For five years, everything gets put on hold.
> Ok...
> It's a pretty big sacrifice. It's difficult to maintain social connections, friendships because it's all time-consuming and the thing we have the least of is time.

Other people, interviewed several months into their mandate, confirmed the importance of work but were less pessimistic about its impact on their personal lives. Whether enthusiastic or defeatist, they all had to learn time management in a situation where time is a rare commodity. The situation is simple; being present in one place means being absent in any number of other possible locations where you could have been and where your absence might be criticized. So, at each moment, each choice must be optimal. This situation holds true for other high-level politicians: Lefebvre, who studied this population in the north of France, also described this quest for time maximization. He wrote, "for politicians, time is rare resource, every second counts even if it is not counted. They must manage a limited time-capital to succeed with the numerous constraints their role puts on them" (Lefebvre, 2014, p. 57).

These intense rhythms, these "weeks full up from Monday to Sunday," and this "life of work," none of this should be a surprise for these novice MPs. After all, the house elected in 2017 was made up of many senior managers, busy professionals, small business owners, or a retailers, all of whom are used to these kinds of rhythms. So why was there this series of protests when they arrived at the Assembly? This leads us to refine the classic analyses about the pace of politics. In focusing too closely on the frenetic nature of political activity and the general shortage of time, researchers overlook another aspect that is at least as important, although less spectacular: the dilated nature of political time. Time certainly stretches in politics, but it is not always intense. This became clear to me through weeks of observation: hectic periods are followed by periods of latency, where the MPs must simply... wait. Although they go from meeting to meeting, sometimes just passing through one to go the next, and although they must attend more appointments and ceremonies than seems humanly possible, they also cannot escape the fact that when they are present, these events take time and they do not always play a central role in them. All too often, their participation is limited to being an official presence and they simply "say a few words."

Cédric Villani, a star mathematician (he won the Fields Medal, the equivalent of a Nobel prize for mathematics) became an MP for LREM. This is what he wrote in his book *Immersion*, which recounts his first steps in the Assembly: "for the first time, I encountered the very special rhythm of political life, alternating long waiting periods and irrepressible emergencies" (Villani, 2019, p. 65). Another first-time MP, Paulin, expressed it equally clearly in an interview:

> What I don't like are the ceremonies, the speeches. It's a total waste of time!
> **Why?**
> Because, you waste an hour with the speeches every time. I think that speeches should be simply the person who has done the thing, who says thanks to everyone for coming. I think sometimes we don't need speeches. Sometimes yes, when there are things... but I prefer to have work meetings than meetings for show where you have to make a speech for five minutes and you say nothing, and if there's ten people who each speak for five minutes, well, you know, it takes an hour and we've all wasted our time.[10]

For these MPs, these constant expectations are not compatible with the injunctions for ubiquity they are also subject to. As a result, they are difficult to deal with. Paulin, a former consultant, expressed this clearly when he described his vision of work. After confiding that he had stopped attending night sessions because "he was exhausted for the rest of the week," he did not mention the intensity of parliamentary work. Instead, he described the *slowness* of time in parliament.

> [Time in parliament?] Oh, it's very slow, yes, when you're sitting there, but when there is a debate on a bill, for the third or fourth time. Because, we've already debated in committee. And then, there's a first debate in the chamber, and then it comes back after the Senate reading, and we redo exactly the same debate, which is exactly the same amendment [...] Well, then, that is tough, and you think, "What is the point?" So, all those things..."[11]

Mathieu, whom we met above, expresses the same complaints regarding ceremonies, another aspect of parliamentarians' work:

> Yes, there are days when it annoys me. The show side of things in particular. It's just not my thing. What I like is files, cases, I like the executive stuff... in any case I like the things that technically push things forward on a concrete level. The side that's ... on display, it's important. But even though I like displays in a public meeting where I feel like I'm contributing something to people, cutting ribbons at ceremonies on the weekend just annoys me.

All these remarks clearly express dissatisfaction, and surprise, with the discovery of this specific temporality of political work. Sometimes very intense, time in parliament can also be extremely slow at others. Political time is ultimately dilated time rather than being systematically fast-paced. It encompasses all of their lives, and slips into each and every moment, but sometimes keeps them waiting for long periods.

In these moments where time slows down, MPs discover what could be described as "parliamentary ennui." After the initial excitement of taking on their new role, they come to realize that their everyday activities are full of repetition, when all that matters is their presence. For novices, the reality of the role comes as quite a shock. "It's something you don't see from the outside" said one; "before, I didn't understand all those photos of the chamber two-thirds empty" says another, who nevertheless acknowledges her frustration at having to attend lengthy sittings to ensure her group has a majority of votes. Discovering the everyday reality of this life, so different from what they imagined, and now committed to the role for a full term, these new MPs feel restricted and are aware that this will last a long time.

The Aristocratic Use of Time

Some MPs I interviewed often talked about their representational functions in pejorative terms, bemoaning the "ribbon cutting and kissing babies circuit," the "nursing home bingo," or the "Olive and Cheese Festival." More than sheer contempt for these activities, they see them as a waste of time in their busy schedule. This impatience denotes a lack of familiarity with political activity, but it also reflects socially situated attitudes toward time. As we have already noted above, the optimization of every moment is a frequent practice among upper classes—the vastly dominant population in parliament—as a result of a socialization that values productivity as well as the number of productive activities. For the upper classes, wasting time is unbearable.

Parliamentary journalist Manon Rescan also noted this trait in her book. She showed that feeling unproductive, or even total uselessness, was much stronger among recently elected former managers and business owners. One former consultant vehemently complained about "having to put up with the slowness in decision-making." Another, also from the private sector, declared, "the night sittings are exhausting. It's the same story, the same people," and this led him to make a suggestion that would further limit the power of parliament: to limit discussion time of the bills. Arguably, he conceded, there is a "logic behind it [which is] democratic and institutional," but he was clearly frustrated to "have to wade through the same discussions dozens of times."[12]

For novice politicians, the discovery of the temporal constraints that weigh on MPs occurs alongside the realization of the limits to the power of MPs. Those who are in opposition often exist exclusively through their interventions in the house, and can do little but comment or propose amendments. And those who are members of the majority are ultimately just as constrained by having to toe the party line. They must vote on the bills that are proposed by the majority, often as quickly as possible—thus with as few interventions as possible. This role as sheer cogs in the passing of government bills is clearest in the sessions where groups of MPs from the majority are essentially under house arrest in parliament on certain evenings or weekends, in order to ensure that the official majority remains numerically present for the vote. These attendance roles, where MPs spend hours voting down amendments by a show of hands, figure clearly in the complaints they confided in me. This is all the more true because for most of them, these novices were, just a few months prior, accustomed to leading rather than being led. Moreover, as the previous chapter demonstrated, they were also called on more often during the first year of their mandate to ensure the majority had sufficient votes.

Clearly, past professional experience plays an important role in attitudes and practices. It leads these MPs to consider the slowness of an activity or their low productivity as time irremediably lost. But to just reduce these complaints to a reflection of upper-class attitudes toward time, and specifically those of private sector managers, would be overlooking an important element. The length of time spent in politics before election, and where it is spent are equally important factors. How well an MP tolerates the waiting imposed by the function is dependent on how used they are to waiting, which means some of their peers not only accept but also appreciate these moments.

These complaints were indeed much less frequent in the interviews I had with MPs who had been in power longer. More accustomed to ceremonies, long deliberations, and the slowness of democracy, they had interiorized these things as normal. Through their participation in events over a period of years, seasoned politicians had learned to wait, and even to like it. The long path to candidacy that many had to take before the 2017 great shortcut, had taught them that there are huge penalties for those who show too much impatience, and substantial rewards for being generous with one's time. An MP must know how to rationalize their work, and thus their time, but they also must be magnanimous with it and show that they are available for the particular population they are visiting at a given moment. If there is some aristocratic legacy in parliamentary representation, it is this use of time: bestowing it ostentatiously, rather than optimizing it at every moment, can be a good investment.

However, the new MPs of 2017 did not know all this, and as a result their experience was very different. The novices who found themselves thrust into the heart of national politics after the 2017 election never got the time to interiorize this specific attitude towards time. Their primary habitus, to borrow the term used by Loïc Wacquant to describe their previously acquired dispositions, was not adapted to the specific needs and expectations of this new parliamentary space, nor were they reshaped by a period in the waiting line (Wacquant, 2011). This contributed to the recurrent accusations they leveled against the Assembly and its "archaic functioning," its time constraints in the first place. The level of frustration was negatively correlated to the time spent in politics. Older MPs, who had been socialized to the time-consuming aspects of their role, had learned to appreciate these moments that are an integral aspect of contemporary politics.

An in-depth analysis of how political time is used would probably show what this ethnographic study suggests, namely that there are gender differences in how MPs use their time. For certain novices, being elected meant competition between family time and political time. They were obliged to be absent for several days a week, which leads to moral dilemmas—particularly for mothers of small children—it is important to note that the male MPs interviewed here did not share this anxiety. Furthermore, they tended to consider this time away from home as a moment of freedom, as being enriching, where their female counterparts tried to conciliate two essentially irreconcilable timetables. This gender gap most likely has an impact on happiness in one's mandate and may explain why some women refused proposals for promotion within the party or the assembly (because it would have meant being away even more). Traditional gender roles seem to still weigh heavy on the women elected in 2017. But this is not the only point where gender has an impact. In interactions with the public, which the novices discovered when they arrived, gender also played a role.

Becoming Public Property

MPs cannot be in two places at once. At best, if they cannot attend an event or invitation, they can delegate some task to their deputy, or more often to a staffer. However, they do have a public image, a kind of double of themselves, which circulates and which they only partially control. This duality of politicians, with one being the physical person and the other their public face, was a discovery for most first-time MPs. After the initial surprise of the first media articles documenting *them*, those who were not accustomed to this realized that being well-known means being recognized, and thus scrutinized, judged, and commented on.

All the interviews said they experienced this, to different extents depending on their exposure. One talked about how people now came up to her in the street when she was walking with her children. Another mentioned how voters started a conversation about his musical tastes, which led him to realize that he needed to better secure his online profiles on various social networks. Many MPs said they were regularly approached by people in their constituencies, sometimes as close as in the stairs of their building. One MP recalled with humor that the "doors [of his building] would open, as though by coincidence, as soon as I left my apartment."

This change in their public status came as a surprise for many. It brought about a shift in the boundaries between public and private, between work life and home life. It also reinforced the feeling of not belonging, and many learned to adapt to it. Some of these adaptations are banal. They consist in changes in the way they dress in public, or increased control over what information is available online. One first-time MP recalled, "before, I would sometimes go shopping in shorts or whatever. Now I pay more attention, because I could meet people and there are. . . . When you're a bit a public figure, then you have to be more careful."[13] The MP mentioned above, who was often accosted on his doorstep, ended up moving.

This unexpected question of public image is even more salient in exchanges with journalists. Among novices, the question of attitudes toward the media gave rise to long and ambivalent answers. One the one hand, MPs did cultivate their contact with journalists. They rapidly realized that media visibility is a key aspect of political capital, and an essential condition for the advancement of both careers and important issues they would want to promote. However, media attention comes with its own set of difficulties, hesitations, and complications. In addition to the fact that their private lives were suddenly public, new MPs discovered that their image was out of their control, and that they could be represented or even quoted in ways they considered as completely unfair and still not be able to do a thing about it.

For many, the first weeks at the assembly were quite brutal in this respect, particularly given that the medias' favorite theme for this new legislature was the blunders made by these novices unaccustomed to the rules of politics or the institution. In this highly mediatized context, where more and more journalists patrolled the corridors, mistakes—even the smallest ones—rarely went unnoticed. Worse, they were often caught on film and circulated widely, like the MP who forgot to cut her microphone just at the moment she decided to criticize her colleagues, or another who was overcome by stress and completely lost his composure when he had to ask his first question to the government, in front of all of his colleagues. For many new MPs, the natural reaction was to distance themselves from the media, at least for a time.

Even when they are familiar with journalistic codes, media attention is often accompanied by something MPs remain sensitive to—being contacted via social network or email. Most often such contacts are negative, and for many, each appearance in the media is accompanied by direct criticism, and sometimes insults. Paulin, the MP who was formerly a consultant, is not a complete novice. He was active in a local section of the Socialist Party, and he was even elected as a municipal councilor for a time. Yet he expressed a feeling of bitterness following his appearances on TV shows and the reactions they provoked:

> But what is true is that I was in the media a lot in December and every time I received torrents of insults. On Twitter, on Facebook, by email. It was very violent. I didn't go public with it because that's not my style. But it's true that in spite of everything, it gets to you. [...] Of course, you protect yourself,

you say well, it's just because it was me on TV, if it had been someone else it would have been the same. And yeah, obviously they get you where you're sensitive, about what you're representing.[14]

Violence in politics is not a new phenomenon. Its evolution is hard to measure, and it is impossible to conclude that it has risen steadily in recent decades. Notwithstanding that, there was a surge during and following the Yellow Vest movement in France around 2019, which saw relatively unknown MPs being verbally aggressed, sometimes outside their homes. After all, in a not-so-distant past, this violence was more visible, surgeries could be boarded up, insults inside the chambers flew from one side to the other, and in Paris a duel even took place (in 1967) between two MPs. By comparison, today's politics seems more appeased. But there has been a change, with the increasing use of social networks that create the possibility for unmoderated, unmediated interaction. It is easier and cheaper to send a message on a social network than to send a letter or physically go to a constituency office—and it is apparently anodyne. Yet as is well known, verbal attacks via this kind of media have become commonplace. They are often less spectacular than physical confrontations, but they are constant. Every day can bring its share of criticism about an MP's political actions, but may also focus on their physical appearance, moral character, clothing, and so on.

The Internet has another consequence, which is that part of what was considered one's private life can become public.[15] Many MPs saw aspects of their life being commented on social networks once they were elected. Others had traces of their past surface, often to be used against them. There was, of course, all sorts of amateur "opposition research" carried out by private citizens or militants from opposition parties. Searching through the tracks the new MPs had left on the Internet, they tried to uncover incriminating assertions, or previous declarations that stood in contradiction to their current positions. Private matters were unearthed too. One novice MP had previously taken an employer before the labor courts, because she was accusing him of not having paid the full remuneration she was entitled to. What could have remained a private dispute became a public controversy after the local newspaper published a series of articles on the case. She was depicted in a very unflattering light, her public profile being used to portray her as some sort of Goliath lashing out against a small organization, even though she considered she was the one who had been defrauded:

Personally, I found it difficult, because everything private became public. Everything. And even things from before. When you're within your rights, it's particularly difficult, really unfair. Above all, because it was portrayed as "this privileged MP who demands extortionate amounts of money from a poor little non-profit." For family, those close to you, it's difficult.

Why?

Because we have the same name, and its everywhere in the media, presented in a negative light. It has a negative impact, it affected me. To the extent where at one point, I just kept my head down. I even hesitated to go to meetings with the mayors. And then when I did go, I felt obliged to begin by saying "you have perhaps heard rumours, but they aren't true." But in the street, I had the feeling everyone was looking at me.[16]

This example is striking and shows the discomfort created by this publicity, and how it can affect one's everyday life, and that of one's family. It is worth noting that first time MPs are not the only political novices to experience this. At the same time that I was conducting this research, the Yellow Vest movement emerged. This protest, which started off against a proposal to increase tax on gas but ended up bringing together individuals from very different walks of life or political opinions, had another distinctive trait: most of its leaders were not familiar with conventional politics. Partly built on a rhetoric opposing elites and the people, it saw other types of newcomers become public figures. Yet the reaction to the rapid publicization was strikingly similar. Located on the exact opposite of the political spectrum, several leaders of the Yellow Vest movement also recounted the extent and the violence of the comments that their public statements provoked—for the most part from people they did not know. For them too, emerging into public view involved receiving a torrent of speeches and comments about themselves, most of them negative. This was not without consequences, and some confessed that they withdrew from an organizing role to avoid such pressure.

Any study of a "spoiled identity"—to borrow from Erving Goffman (1967)—needs to be accompanied by an analysis of how individuals adapt to a new situation. In various texts, the Canadian sociologist analyzed the ways in which individuals adapt to attacks on their public identity. A powerful vector for the normalization of this situation of abnormal exposure involves accepting the new rules of the game. This process is exactly what a journalist who was following them daily described when I mentioned this point to her:

There was one MP who told me, "What's happening at the moment [tensions experienced during the first year], that is interesting because we're learning. We're at a key turning point where, either you become cynical, or you give up." "Giving up, that means accepting that you'll do your five-year term and then throw in the towel, because it's not for you." He said that [to stay in politics], you have to have a form of cynicism because they are constantly being criticized.[17]

Another novice said,

It's changed already in one year. Before, when I received an inflammatory letter, I was sick about it. Now I just say, "whatever, okay." I still answer it, but it doesn't affect me so much. And I think that it will affect me less and less. MPs who have already had a previous mandate easily distance themselves from it. From their role, from the oppositions, from those who are disgruntled. It doesn't pollute them as much; it doesn't take up their time like it does for us.[18]

This kind of disconnection between the person and the *persona*—the public face of the individual—is the result of a process, rather than its explanation. The distinction progressively happens as politicians no longer pay attention to these incidents. But those with more experience expressed their incomprehension or even contempt at the reactions of their new colleagues. This was the case for Martin. When I met him, he was in his 30s, and he already had been active in politics since his time at Sciences Po, either as a party member or as regional councilor. He even did a short time as an adviser in a ministerial cabinet—but despite his best effort, he was not elected to the assembly in 2017. When I discussed the difficulties mentioned by the novices with him, he told me they were "naive" or "hadn't adapted."[19] He considered this publicity to be inherent to the world of politics, thereby naturalizing it, and he looked down on those who complained about it.

This is precisely what Goffman was talking about when he mentioned the different strategies for managing attacks on one's identity. In politics, it involves accepting what is presented as the unavoidable nature of the situation. Other strategies are possible, and they were used, whether the MPs depersonalized the attack ("it is not me who is being attacked"), or whether they discredited their critiques ("we only ever receive complaints," or "most of those who complain are crazy"). Those with experience play an essential role because they provide support for the MPs on an everyday basis, confirming that such attacks are banal.

Officials, and above all staffers, are essential to an MP's socialization to their new role. They are closest to the MP and available to guide them and help them. That is true in all circumstances, but particularly for first time MPs. But here again, novices were not the best prepared for this. Since they did not know about the discreet though essential role of staffers, they were late to the recruitment fair and were not able to get those with experience. They hired friends, fellow party members, but most were novices like themselves. It is only later, when they compare themselves with their more experienced colleagues that they understand the importance of experienced staffers.[20]

Accepting the public gaze and its negative aspects also involves accepting the idea that political action is meaningful, in other words that "it's worth all the effort." This most often occurs via a rationalization process in which the issues they defend are seen as bigger than themselves as individuals, and that justice will ultimately be done later. This belief in the higher value of their action is nothing more than what Bourdieu called *illusio*, the idea that the benefits promised by the activity are desirable. In the face of sometimes hostile conditions, this belief is necessary to maintain engagement. This specific resocialization to the rule of the political games, with its specific totems and taboos, was also lacking in novices. More than any other MPs in interviews, they questioned the relevance of their action, or whether they should pursue a political life. Hence the role of rituals, such as the group meeting on Tuesday morning, in which members of government regularly participate; or the lunches regularly organized between ministers and MPs—these moments of "communication" or "coordination" are in fact programs that foster novice MPs' belief in the work they do, even in the face of violent events.

Striking Blows and Making Deals

Mikhail Bakhtin once wrote, "at every point in its historic existence, language is stratified internally." According to the Russian literary theorist, it is divided into a series of "generational" or "social dialects," or again "profession jargons" (Bakhtin, 1981, pp. 290–291). Each of these sociolects—Bakhtin did not use that term, it would be introduced later—is thus specific to a particular group. Clearly, politics has its own idiolect. For instance, during my interviews I was introduced to the term "*popole*." It refers to a certain conception of political activity, understood as being a game of strategy, a series of transactions and exchanges that are well understood and serve to pursue a specific goal. "*Faire de la popole*" [doing popole] means negotiating or taking a shot at one's ultimate end—whether those shots are well-understood exchanges, or an indirect strategy described as accepting a small deal as a first step toward a big one. Unlike its closest English equivalent ("politicking") it is so specific to the political field that it would be understood by everyone in that sphere, but would be almost completely unknown for those outside politics.

Even though the novices who arrived in 2017 did not know the term, they could not overlook this image of political activity. Countless TV productions are dominated by a vision of politicians as strategic, cynical, even scheming individuals. This image sometimes serves as the main narrative trope. The US television show *House of Cards*, about Washington, the main character played by Kevin Spacey, embodies all these clichés about politicians to the point of caricature. More generally, this portrayal of politics as a combat sport is widespread. But having a vague idea that politics might be like this is not the same thing as experiencing it for yourself.

From this point of view, many of the novices interviewed expressed their frustrations about the way politics is conducted. Martine, for example, whom we saw above, told me that she was not particularly interested in focusing on strategies, especially when this type of thinking took over conversations or the way the work was organized. One day in 2019, as I was interviewing her (as I had done regularly since her first day in office), this usually soft-spoken woman launched into a rant about her party's electoral strategy. "I don't understand what they are doing," she raged. She went on to explain that in the previous weeks, her party had begun to approach local politicians in her region to prepare for the upcoming municipal elections. These were seen as crucial for LREM, since the still recent party was trying to establish itself locally. But according to her, most of the conversations revolved around the electoral potential of the candidates, not their political ideology. "They do things backward," she complained. "We don't even have a shared platform, or a charter of values we can ask them [possible new candidates] to agree on." She then said tersely that she would have preferred them to start with this shared program, "otherwise we will attract opportunists."[21] Visibly, neither the leaders of the majority nor the prime minister, whom she spoke to about this during a meeting, considered it problematic.

To prioritize strategies may have looked surprising to her, but it was widely accepted, and also defended, by some of her colleagues. Aurelie, Another MP also elected for the first time, was by no means a novice when I met her. At age 30, she had already been active in politics for 15 years. In our interview, she expressed her regret that the majority was not "more political." By this she meant being able to make this kind of arrangement saying, "the older MPs all say it. They say, 'let us do deals,' 'let us do play politics,' 'we want more politicking, we don't do it anymore.'" When I asked her what she meant she quoted a French television show which focuses, like other political TV series, on the trials and tribulations of politicians in accessing power at any price. "It is the *Baron Noir*[22] side of things, the strategy, I'll scratch your back if you scratch mine. I think that's really interesting because, in the end, the goal is to get an idea voted in." She also regretted that now "You don't see it much. There are a few, those who are close to the Elysée"—a synecdoche for the first circle around the president—"who can do it, and they do it directly with the Ministers. But that's what, like a dozen MPs, that's all."[23]

This strategic attitude toward politics impacts not only behaviors but also discourses and the way politicians talk about their actions. One political journalist I spoke to complained about a young novice MP from the majority who was "still unable to *talk politics*" in interviews, despite "the different phases of media training" (training program for communication in the media) she has gone through. When I asked this journalist what he meant by "talk politics," he gave me a loose definition revolving around the idea of "exposing power struggles," stating that "there are some who don't know how to talk the language of politics. They talk about content, about a subject, and that's it."[24] Talking politics, for the political journalists who are as seasoned as the long-time politicians, means being willing to talk about strategies, backstage maneuvers, and power struggles.

This presentation of politics as a place of conflict therefore thus doesn't stem only from the MPs themselves, nor their staffers. It is a common understanding shared by many. This is a sign that politics is a world that is also structured by expectations that exist prior to the arrival of newcomers. Parliamentary journalists have long established rituals that allow them to obtain information. One of them is the classic "lunch group." Generally, 4 to 6 participants attend these private, invitation-only, events. The journalists, who work for different outlets, constitute the core of the group and they invite an MP of their choice for an entirely "off the record" conversation with them. The goal of these sessions is to provide the journalists with background information on the ongoing affairs in parliament, which will be used in future articles—with the implicit understanding that no one will be named. Through these events, journalists gain access to rumors and insights into internal power struggles. MPs, for their part, cultivate the good graces of several journalists, and they command their attention for over an hour.[25]

Asked about these lunch groups in the new Assembly, the journalists' comments were unanimous. They overwhelmingly regarded novices as terrible guests for these politicking rituals—which such lunches are. This same journalist, who had been covering parliament for a decade or so, told me in July 2018:

> For us, the most complicated group to follow is LREM. Among them, there are really a lot of people who were not used to political codes, who didn't want to talk about politics in terms of conflicts. But for us, at [he cites the name of his newspaper] that's what we sell. We need this politicking. I can't sell parliamentary debate to my readers. So, it's a problem. Novices are very reticent to talk about anything except their specific subjects. They don't read things in the same way, so they don't necessarily see.[26]

This extract shows the expectations of some of the political journalists. They are used to describing politics as a series of inter- and intraparty battles in which MPs and parties pursue strategic oppositions in order to gain power. But they also show that one of the reasons these norms persisted was because of the expectations of peripheral actors, such as journalists. The large-scale renewal of the political class following the election did not change the fact that the various people they interact with all remained in place, thus contributing to the inertia of their environment, and to their normalization.

These two visions of what it means to "do politics" are illustrated in this conflict, which Aurélie relates, involving an exchange with a novice colleague.

> I'll tell you an anecdote. We had a meeting in parliament, organized by the national train company and the cabinet [of the president of her region], because there is a project for a new train line [. . .] Sitting at the table were the representative of the company, some aides to the region president, and me and my colleagues—both MPs from the region. The SNCF [the train company] presented the project, it was very technical, and the cabinet of the president of the region began to whine. And I could hear the underlying message, which was that the project wasn't progressing as they wanted,

partly because they thought it was blocked by the transport minister [in the same party as Aurélie and her colleague].

So I took the floor and I thanked them [...]. and I said, "However, given you are busy politicking, I will respond in kind. Perhaps if the region had not completely blocked the bill [proposed by the government on a different subject], this topic would have fared better." And I explained to them perhaps that was why the relationship was more complicated than with other regions. And then we started talking politics: we talked about this reform, about the train line, about the region.

But at this point my colleague stopped us and said [she mimics a nasal whiny voice with an air of stupidity] "Oh, will you stop! I'm here for a technical meeting, I'm not here for party politics!" Can you imagine? She said, "I'm not here for politics." So, I burst out, and I said, "Come off it! You're an MP, if you're not here for politics, what ARE you here for?" A silence ensued, and she went all red and she left.[27]

The example is telling, and it dovetails with established results—both about politics as a world of jabs and taunts and about the diverging practices between novices and professionals already noted by Wilson half a century ago (Wilson, 1962). However, although we can clearly see two opposing visions of politics here—one that prioritizes deals through conflict and exchange, and the other that emphasizes common interest—it would be caricatural to consider that those who favor politicking do so only in their own interest, because they seek visibility or re-election. Of course, this motive is not entirely absent, but a more accurate description is that Aurélie also believes that is how good politics should be conducted. In that sense, the reason she criticized her colleague is that she saw her as incapable of moving issues forward, that she lacked political know-how—which for Aurélie and her like-minded peers justified these strategic exchanges. This idea was expressed several times in the interviews, for example by this MP in his 30s whom I met once over lunch. He had recently been elected for the first time, but he had substantial previous experience. He had work as an adviser in several ministerial cabinets, after having been employed as a party employee for the youth branch of the Socialist Party. He explained that he had trouble understanding "those colleagues who think that politics is just about having a good idea," and he went on to expound his vision of how to be successful, both in terms of projects and career. To him, strategy was key.

What came out of these interviews is the idea that politics is built around strategic action. This requires having a clear target, and sometimes taking shots at your colleagues. As I was asking about friendships in parliament, Aurélie replied that she had no friends here, but also that she did not plan to have any. "It is not possible, politics is a world of sharks! It's hard! You have to toughen up [...] and it is rare to make friends within the majority, you have to know that! Some thought they were going to make a bunch of friends... well no!" When I asked why, she replied tersely, "because there will necessarily come a time when you're in competition with each other."

Mathieu, the former senior civil servant, was more nuanced, yet he described the same thing when he talked about the explicitly competitive relationships he discovered in the Assembly. Although long, this excerpt is worth quoting in full because it both provides a precise documentation of the situation, but it also identifies the primary actors in it—political insiders.

> You quickly realize that some people are not playing a collaborative game. During the campaign, everyone was pulling together, we were shooting against the same enemies. Not so much after the election. If I return to my comparison with my previous job, I'd say that it's a bit like an all-out war here at the Assembly. There's always some ulterior motive, and it's not always easy to understand the logic. It's always a shifting game of alliances, and so you go from the phase of the campaign where there's a friendly unanimity, to a moment where everyone realizes that we will be in competition, even if we're on the same team, and sometimes it's quite brutal.
>
> I don't think that I'm responsible for that kind of behavior, but there are some, those who have more experience, sometimes it's pretty heavy going. They'll stoop to anything to nab things that sometimes seem completely secondary. And which are secondary, in fact, in terms of how this assembly functions. But the "whatever commission," the position of "secretary in this or that committee," and for that they're capable of anything, so they can make their little contribution, or hit their milestone in their political career. It's quite something when you go from a campaign where it's all rose-colored, to a world that becomes really political, in the sense of getting and keeping hold of power, in the Machiavellian sense, and that comes in quite quickly I mean. In the two months that followed, you can see those who have managed to make that shift and those who haven't [...]
>
> **And you said that those who were the most comfortable with this, were the people who had experience in politics?**

They are the ones who knew the rules, and who are much more cunning, in Machiavellian terms. So there are lots of people who come in with a great deal of goodwill, who want to work together, to collaborate as they did during the campaign, and who realize, to their astonishment—once again it's not really the case for me because in administration it's more comfortable but still just as violent—who realize that it's not friendly anymore, things are more political, so with more power relations—and there are MPs for whom this comes as a complete shock.

It is difficult to think of a discourse more opposed to that of the "benevolence" mentioned by Macron during his campaign, this idea that politics can be done openly, without underhand blows. This idea of "honest politics" was often quoted in the first months of the mandate by first-time MPs from LREM, as an ideal that had attracted them. But soon it was no longer mentioned by anyone.

The image of a violent world in which anything is permitted in pursuit of one's ends is such a stereotype that we have to wonder whether it is not a kind of official narrative served up to outsiders. There are many reasons why someone could use such a trope, be it out of laziness, to emphasize their personal resistance or their status in the face of such a challenge, or simply to set themselves apart from the rest. But the major shift that took place in 2017 provided another way to test this hypothesis. Indeed, when the wave of novices arrived in the Assembly in 2017, that meant many former MPs had to leave. And with them went a substantial portion of their teams who were not able to keep a foot in politics, be it as party officials or as staffers. A long interview with one of them, a staffer who had an important role working for a visible MP in the previous legislature, confirmed this. This young woman in her 30s was now working as a lobbyist. When I interviewed her a year later, she mentioned her surprise at the level of constraint involved in the interactions in her new professional sphere. According to her, there was a sharp contrast between her old and her new life:

> I have progressively come to realize things. For example, I was with my sister one night [who is a manager in a large company] and she was saying that she had to reprimand one of her employees, because of how she spoke to the staff. And I was thinking that in politics, you're rude and disrespectful all the time. I realized that I myself spoke down to people. But in other

spheres, that isn't possible, it isn't acceptable [. . .] In hindsight, I realized that the level of violence was incredibly high [in politics].

When I asked her again about the violence she said she experienced, she explained:

> So, I found myself thrust up against a wall in a corridor with an MP screaming in my face that "you don't do stuff like that," or more or less explicit threats like "I'm going to bust your knees." People do notice, they say, "that's not good," but it goes on anyway [. . .]
> And then there's moral violence, everyday interactions that are much more tense and stressful than elsewhere. You're either talking down to people or you're screaming at them, the brutality of the interactions is much stronger and that's normal.
> **And you didn't realise?**
> In fact, you're like the proverbial frog in boiling water, you don't realize what's happening until you explode.[28]

An in-depth study should analyze the reasons for the prevalence of violence in its different forms. A tentative sociological explanation of this climate which is often described as an "all-out war" would probably involve an analysis of the organizational form of professional politics. The intensity of interactions in this world is probably partly due to the fact that political leaders—particularly if they want to make a career—must be constantly conscripting people to their cause without necessarily having hierarchical authority over them. It is rare that MPs have enough staff, and they can never have enough support. Most of their work consists in garnering support from people to whom they can only offer promises. Combined with the fact that politics is a highly time-consuming activity in which public and private boundaries are at best blurry and at worst nonexistent, this might pave the way for an explanation as to why politics appears to be so bellicose, a world in which anything goes. Rather than considering it an essential character trait of this world, or those who inhabit it, we would benefit from seeing it as the result of specific material organization.

***

In autumn of 2018, the Yellow Vest movement began. The initial protest against increased taxes on diesel rapidly made way for a much wider range of claims. It also made its way into the public space through a series of people who, like the LREM novices, had never had any experience of national politics. And although these two groups are very different socially and politically, their experiences may be similar. This was the case for Ingrid Levavasseur, a young single mother and hospital worker who quickly became one of the spokespeople for this multifarious movement, and was as a result regularly invited to speak on talk shows and in the media over a period of months. In hindsight, she mentioned the "violence" of the exchanges she experienced. This included comments made about her by strangers; violence from journalists or political figures who debated with her; but violence also in relations within the movement. One day, while she participated in a street demonstration, she was violently set upon and had to be exfiltrated. Shortly afterward, she withdrew from the movement and stopped all her public activities.

Although it is frequently condemned, violence against political representatives is not new. Rather, it has come in waves. But novices felt it much more deeply than their seasoned counterparts. They were shaken in their beliefs, affected on a personal level. There is a reason for that, and once again it has to do with the political waiting line. In addition to socializing aspiring politicians to these norms of interaction, it also offers a time to weed out those who are not willing to face its violence. During the time they spend waiting, these potential candidates have a chance to leave. Because it functions as a conservative device, the waiting line preserves the individuals who are the most suited to the functioning of the political field. Those who are the least well equipped to manage this violence are the first victims of it, and once they have realized that, they may decide to not go into politics or to get out very quickly. The following chapter pursues this reflection on self-selection and self-exclusion, conducted within a very different group, the elite upper classes. Starting from them, it investigates why—despite these tough conditions—people enter, and then cling to, a career in politics.

5
THE PASSION FOR POLITICS

Some terms just do not fit well together. For example, talking about hardship at work for politicians would undoubtedly raise some eyebrows. Indeed, the general criticism of MPs is so strong that evoking any of their potential difficulties in the workplace is generally met with sarcasm. Yet doctors, psychologists, or even staff representatives would have much to say about their working conditions. And although those conditions remain more comfortable than those of many other workers, and therefore should not inspire pity, they are nevertheless far from ideal. All the actors in the field recognize this; in the words of two US consultants, "Politics is a world of taunts, jeers, jabs, pointed fingers and mudslinging [. . .] Fear, anger, envy, indignation and shame are powerful emotions in the political arena. [. . .] Negative campaigning is rarely pretty. Sometimes it doesn't feel very good either" (Schlackman & Douglas, 1995, p. 25). That this quote is about the US system, or about consultants who have spent their lives "living off politics" without ever being elected does not make it any less relevant; on both sides of the Atlantic the situation is the same. Ironically enough, the labor code is almost never applied to those who write it: politicians are essentially unprotected from abuses in this area. The vocational nature of their profession means that MPs accept much more hectic working conditions than their fellow citizens and they avoid the rare health and safety barriers in place. The expectations placed on them are significant—because of their specific roles, they ought to behave as exemplary individuals, whose daily life is never under investigation. But the fact they are "ill-reputed" does nothing to help normalize their work. More is expected of them, and above all they are expected to not complain.

Despite this, politics is not an occupation that is in want of candidates. The most prestigious positions are always highly sought after. The primaries of the major parties, introduced around 15 years ago, have not been very effective at limiting the number of candidates, and the disintegration of the traditional parties seems to have paved the way for ever more numerous individual initiatives. But less directly visible positions are also coveted. The number of candidates at the legislative level has also increased steadily over the last three decades (at least), as have town councilors at the municipal level—France boasts some 500,000 municipal council positions, which are almost always filled after hotly contested elections.

Yet, survey after survey shows that politics is the most unpopular professional activity for French people—politicians are less prestigious than journalists, tax collectors, or even ticket controllers on the Parisian metro.

Exploring the reasons for this apparent paradox means allowing for the possibility of responses that reiterate the very negative image of MPs. One common interpretation is that MPs are motivated by monetary interests—if these positions are so desired, it is because they are highly lucrative. It is true that with a monthly net income of close to €5,700, an MP in France earns more than 97% of the active population, and those serving as ministers may earn twice as much again. According to those who support this interpretation, multiple office holding also needs to be considered. Although it is virtually impossible to hold multiple elected positions today, as the practice is now strictly regulated, this practice is still present in the minds of voters. And then there are the spin-off careers, that see former politicians offered very lucrative positions in the private sector once their mandate is over. There is no shortage of examples here, sometimes even at the highest echelons of the state. Recently, the former French prime minister and ill-fated presidential hopeful, François Fillon, and the former German chancellor Gerhard Shröder, both accepted positions in Russian corporations. They joined the long list of former dignitaries who profit from the contacts and knowledge they acquired working during their time in power.

This interpretation is frequent even in scientific and academic circles. The theme of MPs' self-interest underpins a significant amount of research—in political economics of course, but often other areas too. Although it might appear self-evident, this interpretation faces a series of "anomalies"—following Thomas Kuhn's definition of events that disturb the dominant paradigm of an era. Indeed, although French MPs undeniably make a good living, many of them would have earned similar salaries, or even more, in the private sector. Moreover, as we show in this chapter, 30 years of constant decline in MPs' living conditions did not prevent La République en Marche (LREM) MPs (among whom higher socioeconomic categories were highly overrepresented) from running en masse in 2017.

Could it be then that the men and women who aspire to a career in politics do so for the prestige? Once again, we will explore the evidence in support of this often-mentioned hypothesis, but it is worth immediately stressing that it does not seem very plausible either. The surveys discussed above on the perception of politicians, as well as the role of the parliament in France seem to suggest otherwise.

How can we explain this attraction of politics, without assuming that it is irrational? And if politics is seen in such a negative light and they could earn good money elsewhere, why would politicians bother? Once again, an explanation in terms of the waiting line helps us understand the logic of their commitment, but also why they persist in this physically demanding and morally degraded position. During their waiting period a selection occurred, during which only the most motivated stayed. MPs—particularly those who waited the longest—were socialized to political activity and how it operates. They learned to love the pace, the randomness, the challenges. They developed a passion for politics that for them outweighs all the negative associations this position might have in the eyes of the rest of society.[1]

This chapter provides a sociological reading of a practice that is more frequently interpreted either in terms of pure self-interest or is otherwise pathologized. Indeed, there is no shortage of terms to describe the "addiction" MPs are said to suffer from, their dependency on the drug of politics. Rather than following these descriptions which ultimately have limited explanatory power, we will focus on what gets these MPs "hooked," and specifically on what they consider unique about this work. By focusing on the ways in which these MPs "see" and "do" politics, what drives them forward, and what they miss when they leave, this chapter aims to contribute to the analysis of this oft-evoked passion for politics.

Decreasing Returns

Work More to Earn Less

Every day of the week, whether parliament is in session or not, an endless ritual occurs in front of this old building overlooking the Seine, in the very prestigious 7th arrondissement of Paris. Every 15 minutes, dozens of people embark on a tour of the French parliament. During their visit, they learn about the history of the Palais-Bourbon, which was originally built on land known as the Pré-au-Clercs, which was once a peripheral area with a bad reputation. Because few people lived there, it was also known as a place where duels could be held. Construction on the main building of the palace began in 1722 at the initiative of the duchess of Bourbon, the legitimized daughter of King Louis XIV and his mistress, Madame de Montespan. The future Princess de Condé had bought the land, which she gave to her lover the Marquis de Lassay, who built a stately mansion on it. The Palais Bourbon and the Hôtel de Lassay today respectively constitute the main buildings of the lower house of parliament, and the residency of the President of the Assembly. Up until the French Revolution, they remained the property of the dukes of Condé, but have since been almost exclusively used to house the national representatives.

As they walk through the ballrooms, visitors discover these historic spaces, the antechambers, and the inner courtyards of the Hôtel de Lassay. If parliament is in session, they will most likely encounter MPs in the room of the *Quatre Colonnes*, this often-crowded interface between the private spaces of parliament and those open to journalists. But if the chamber is empty, the visitors may take a look beyond this "sacred perimeter," normally sealed off by bailiffs. They explore the Delacroix room (known as "the left's room" because of its position in relation to the chamber), and the Pujol room ("the right's room"). They also pause in the Casimir-Périer room, to admire a monumental bronze fresco created by Dalou, and finally they enter the chamber itself. Throughout the visit, the guide explains the organization of parliamentary life, through history up to today. Today's MPs are part of a long line of representatives which began with the first National Constituent Assembly in 1789 and which can be traced over two hundred years of history up until today.

Yet behind the apparently immutable appearance of the institution and its rituals, there are many differences in parliamentary practice. This is of course true of the different regimes that have given parliament pride of place over the years. If we specifically look at the postwar period, the contrast between the Fourth and the Fifth Republic is particularly striking. The Constitution of October 4, 1958, which marked passage to the Fifth Republic with the return of General de Gaulle, meant a transfer of power from the parliament to the executive. Even though the constitutional regime is still the same today, the practice of parliamentary politics is now quite different. In fact, the entire atmosphere and organization of the parliament has evolved dramatically, from a small and somewhat antiquated political world to a stage for unrelenting media exposure.

Rather than just being different, parliamentary work is above all more much constrained than it used to be. In terms of legislation and control, parliamentary activity has increased steeply since the beginning of the Fifth Republic. This can be seen in the number of parliamentary sessions per year, a figure that has risen sharply from 120 sessions per year at the beginning of the Fifth Republic, to more than 300 sessions today. Expressed as a number of days, parliament now regularly sits more than 130 days a year, more than one in three. Given that at least half of the week is dedicated to work in the constituency, this means that there is little useful time that is not spent in session.

Expectations regarding the presence of MPs in Paris have also clearly increased. One MP, elected in 1978 as part of the right-wing majority and who still held his seat in 2012, put it like this:

> MPs are more present than they were when I first arrived. When I was first elected, I remember that [Jacques] Chirac, who was the president of the RPR back then, welcomed us here. In essence, he said, "congratulations you have been wonderful. Now I don't want to see you here anymore" (*laughs*). He was obviously addressing new MPs above all, saying, "I don't want to see you here because if you want to be re-elected next time, you'll have to dig yourself into your constituency. So, get going. Don't worry about what happens here, go see your voters.[2]

It is not that MPs in the 1960s had six months holiday a year between the two parliamentary sessions. Committees could meet outside of these sessions and the constituency work was ongoing. However, it is certain that the timetables of the MPs were less busy than they are now. This was so true that many of them maintained another activity alongside their political position. Some worked as professionals, others cumulated elected offices. The increase in the volume of work, combined with the obligation to attend weekly sessions, makes this kind of double activity more complicated today. MPs interviewed in the 2010s who had another profession before being elected, had trouble maintaining that profession afterward. This is all the more true as the rules governing extraparliamentary activities have become much stricter over time.

Moreover, in recent decades there has been increasing control and surveillance over allocation expenses. For example, it is now no longer possible to directly employ one's partner or children, a situation that had led to widespread abuse and scandals. The most famous of these scandals was the one that hit the campaign of the 2017 right-wing candidate for the presidency, François Fillon, and assuredly contributed to his electoral loss. However, the greatest change to French political careers in recent times was undoubtedly the 2014 formal prohibition of multiple office holding. This measure, implemented for the first time in 2017, was intended to ensure that MPs were entirely dedicated to the task of national-level representation. Before this, MPs were able to cumulate their legislative position with other elected offices, such as mayor, or local councilor. It is hard to estimate the full effects of this law, but there is one aspect that is certain, the reform undoubtedly made the position more unstable—and thus less desirable. Combining several mandates (*député-maire*, being an MP and the mayor of a town, was a common one) was a way for MPs to cover their bases in case of electoral defeat. Should they lose one election, they would almost never find themselves unemployed. This is no longer a possibility.

Have these constraints, and the additional working demands, given rise to larger returns? After all, it may be possible that the National Assembly applied the motto coined by former President Nicolas Sarkozy, when he encouraged French people to "work more to earn more." Providing a precise response to this question would require access to the revenues earned by MPs. One might imagine that such information would be readily available in a democracy, but I discovered that this was not the case, at least not in France. Up until very recently, it was hard to know how much French MPs could earn from their work in parliament. France is not the only country where this is the case; in a study conducted with Éric Buge we were able to observe how patchy this information is, particularly if we are looking to obtain a long-term overview of its evolution.

This lack of transparency on the remuneration of MPs—a subject that is fundamental to democracy—can be easily explained, particularly if we adopt the perspective of the parliamentarians themselves. Any discussion on their resources gives rise to a wave of uninterrupted criticism, but this not a new phenomenon. French historian Alain Garrigou has shown, during the debate on the parliamentary indemnities set in 1906, that the question of money is potentially explosive. Even then, when MPs attempted to have the parliamentary allowance bought up to 15,000 francs (instead of the 9,000 it had been set at since the 19th century), there was extensive criticism. Some people criticized the MPs for being venal, others (while recognizing the decline in their standard of living) criticized them for their lack of political savvy. Outside the chamber itself, few defended such a move.

Over the course of the decades that followed, each increase in the parliamentary allowance was followed by accusations that were so heated the MPs did everything to avoid the subject. As André Tardieu, an MP in the Third Republic, wrote in his text *La Profession Parlementaire*, "the general will of elected representatives is that their allowance be mentioned as little as possible. When it comes to increasing the allowance, the vote is conducted in silence and very quickly. The 15,000 francs of 1906 were obtained through a sleight of hand. The following increases were as remote from public debates as possible."[3] One socialist MP, Marcel Coquillaud, who was interviewed on the subject in 1938, said much the same thing when he began with, "this subject is particularly uncomfortable for us."[4] Indeed, over the course of the 20th century, MPs made a lot of effort to not discuss the allowance in public. This probably explains why the question was raised so infrequently. After 1958, there would be almost no mention of the parliamentary allowance. In fact, some work went into ensuring that the issue would be raised as little as possible.

Despite this organized silence, I was able (following lengthy research conducted with my colleague Éric Buge) to produce an estimate of MPs' income. Because it does not take into account the significant differences in MPs' situations, it cannot be anything other than an approximation. In particular, it does not account for the difference between MPs who were allowed to hold multiple elected positions and thus accumulate different sources of revenue, and those who are today prohibited from doing so. However, it does enable us to see how what could be described as a base salary for a French MP has evolved over time.

Once this estimate has been produced, we can compare it to the income of the average French person. Figure 5.1 shows this income estimate in relation to the tax revenue of certain percentiles of the active population.[5] The comparison between the parliamentary allowance and the level of income of various groups in France is highly informative. First, it demonstrates that MPs receive remuneration that is, and has always been, comparatively very high compared to that of French citizens. Even in the years following the First World War, when inflation ate away at the parliamentary allocations that were not reindexed (to do so it would have been necessary to pass a law and thus give in to accusations of self-interest), the allowance still placed them in the most well-paid echelons of French society. Second, from the 1950s up

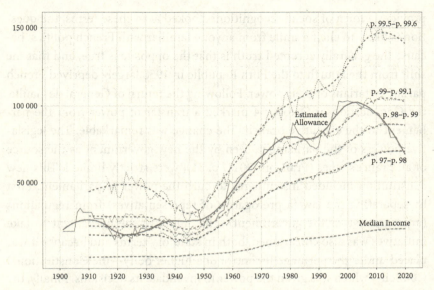

Figure 5.1 Estimated income from holding a parliamentary position in France (1914–2021), and selected percentiles of population income.

until late 1990s, MPs were in fact among the highest earning 1%. Given that a large majority of them combined this allowance with other forms of revenue (most notably as mayors), their total income clearly placed them in the top 1% of the income distribution. But the graph also shows that there has been a clear downward evolution since then. The allowance is still substantial, but it is smaller than it was in the 1990s.

This trend changed in the 2000s. Slowly but surely the income level decreased, with inflation eating away at income that was, as for all French public servants, not readjusted for inflation. Parliamentary allowances decreased to 2% and then 3% of highest earning categories in France. They remain arguably very high, but the decrease was nevertheless as rapid as it was marked.

The Relegation of Parliament

If not by money, could it be possible that the increase in the parliamentary workload is compensated for by a surplus of social prestige? Or that parliamentarians have exchanged monetary returns for a position that provides a form of social recognition? Looked at in these terms, the question is likely to elicit a smile from anyone familiar with French politics, because the generally accepted truth is that the opposite is true, and that the shift from the Fourth to the Fifth Republic in 1958 largely deprived French parliamentarians of their power. Following the return of General de Gaulle, the Constitution of October 4 marked a transfer of power from the parliament to the executive branch. The change was remarkable. The legislative powers of the parliament, seen by the new government as the source of all France's woes (François, 2011, p. 31), were strictly limited. This new constitution included instruments to curb the power of parliament. First by separating the law (a prerogative of representatives) from regulations (a prerogative of the government). The ability of the parliament to take initiatives was also constrained, both in statutory terms and because it was placed under the permanent control of a higher body—the Constitutional Council—which was given the power to invalidate its decisions. Finally, the parliament's control over the government was also curtailed. A government is now unlikely to be overturned by the parliament given how restrictive the conditions for doing so have become. Explicitly designed to put an end to the chronic instability of past regimes, the constitution of 1958 effectively and massively reinforced the power of the executive, at the expense of the legislative branch. Since that date, few would defend the idea that parliament is the main site of political power in France. Of course, there have been variations over the course of this now long Fifth Republic, but the general observation seems clear.

In sociology, a typical way to gauge the decline of institutions consists in analyzing their social make-up. It is a well-known fact that attractive careers draw socially advantaged populations, and those in decline recruit from increasingly disadvantaged groups. If this holds true, then parliamentary politics is an activity "in decline" in France.

From an overall perspective, this decrease is relative, of course. The National Assembly is still overwhelmingly made up of members from the upper classes. In fact, it is even more socially homogeneous in the 2010s than it was before. Between the 1930s and the 1980s, the French Communist Party successfully promoted workers onto the benches of parliament. Although they remained a minority, a dozen, and later a handful of former industrial workers were elected during this period. But with the electoral decline of this party since the late 1980s, along with its own professionalization, this main avenue into parliament for working-class representatives has been lost. But that is not the only change. Another, more subtle yet no less relevant shift is the drop in the number of parliamentarians from the uppermost sections of French society. Between 1978 and 2012 the proportion of those working as liberal professionals in the health sector dropped from 12% to 6%. The number of liberal professionals working in the law has also declined, although this is less dramatic, due to the long-standing possibility for MPs to obtain a degree as a lawyer once their mandate was over. Even more significant is the drop in the number of top civil servants among MPs, from 13.4% to 6.6% (see Table 5.1 below).

The same trend can be seen among graduates of the Ecole National d'Administration (ENA), this incubator for French political and administrative elites. The proportion of MPs who graduated from this highly prestigious administrative school has dropped from 7% to 5% in 40 years. This shift, although minor, should be seen in the context of another change, which is more of a contrast. During the same period, graduates from this prestigious school flocked to political, but nonelected, positions. According to the study conducted by François Denord and Paul Lagneau-Ymonet, in the 1980s, 25% of ENA graduates had a professional experience in a ministerial cabinet less than 10 years after graduating. By the 2000s, this was true of 40% of them (Denord & Lagneau-Ymonet, 2016, p. 139). In other words, although this group remains clearly interested in politics, a career in parliament seemed much less attractive to them in the 2000s than it was to their predecessors.

From the 1970s to the 2010s, there was a shift in the social profile of people running for parliamentary election. This was also demonstrated in other political spaces. Behr and Michon observed the same tendency among the ministers of the Fifth Republic (Behr & Michon, 2015). They noted a decline in what they called "technocrats" (mostly senior civil servants) and an increase in the number of former staffers among MPs. The same kind of phenomena are also at work overseas. In their study of the British political elite, Bovens and Wille show that the proportion of MPs with higher degrees has increased steadily over the last 50 years, but those graduating from prestigious universities has been in constant decline since the 1970s. The proportion of MPs graduating from Oxbridge universities was 36% in 1979 but had dropped to 26% in 2015 (Bovens & Wille, 2017, p. 117). In both Great Britain and the Netherlands, these authors note the progressive withdrawal of aristocrats and social elites from parliament to the benefit of the middle classes (Bovens & Wille, 2017, p. 122).

Table 5.1 Main occupation of MPs in various legislatures, prior to working full-time in politics (as a percentage)

	6th legislature (1978–1981)	11th legislature (1997–2002)	14th legislature (2012–2017)	15th legislature (2017–present)	LREM MPs from the 15th legislature (2017–)	Active population in France (2015)
Farmers	5.0	2.8	2.9	2.6	1.6	1.8
Artisans, shopkeepers, business owners	3.9	5.7	3.7	11.3	14.0	6.4
Managers and professionals	64.0	66.5	57.0	54.7	60.7	17.7
Intermediary positions	14.4	14.1	16.9	13.5	14.0	25.4
Service employees	3.2	0.9	0.8	1.0	0.3	28.1
Workers	6.9	1.5	0.2	0.0	0.0	20.4
Staffers, party permanents, political aides	1.9	8.0	16.4	15.2	8.4	-
Undetermined profession	0.7	0.6	2.1	1.7	1.0	0.0
Total	100.0	100.0	100.0	100.0	100.0	100.0

54.7% of MPs in the 15th legislature listed their primary occupation as managers before their entry into full-time politics.

A Money Problem?

Is the social recruitment that was mentioned above linked to remuneration? A well-known argument, often mentioned in political economics, suggests that there is a direct connection between the two. The idea is that higher salaries allow for the recruitment of people with higher qualifications, and sometimes from higher social groups. But is this link so self-evident? In the French case at least, the connection is far from certain, because in 2017 there was a return of social elites to the Assembly, even though salaries have declined consistently since 2017, and even though the majority MPs announced that they wanted to limit salaries even more in the name of "moralizing political life."

Yet there is another explanation, one that is premised on the idea of waiting line, and that better fits the facts. It is based on the idea that the elites left the Assembly not because work there was not well paid, but because it was complicated to access that work, and particularly to access it quickly. The existence of a waiting period before becoming an MP meant that this career path was long, insecure, and uncertain, where 40 years ago it was quick and straightforward. But with the time required to wait in secondary positions having doubled, this work has become less attractive for social elites. Those who were still highly motivated by politics entered it, but only on its margins, in ministerial cabinets or as civil servants. Others stayed away and took jobs in the private sector.

The interviews conducted with LREM MPs who moved into electoral politics in 2017 clearly show that salary was only one aspect of a more general decision, and probably not the most important one. One LREM MP expressed this explicitly. With a background in the Socialist Party, he above all focused on the long path toward positions of power in politics in the 2010s:

> Was I expecting to get elected? Before that date [2017] I couldn't. Because when you're not part of a traditional system, with traditional nominations, you can't take that career path. Deep down, I think I would have always liked to be a parliamentarian, but it was never concretely formulated in my head.
>
> **Why is that?**
>
> Because in the Socialist Party, you have to be faithful to your local branch, so you have to be elected to the branch Bureau of your, party and you have to make sacrifices for several years, and then eventually hope to be

nominated by the party—but at what age? And even if this is the case, you will first be a candidate in a constituency that it is impossible to win, and only later in one that is possible, and then one day maybe you will make it to parliament. That's it. That's the life of a traditional parliamentarian. So, of course, that wasn't on my horizon. Me, I had my career in the private sector, I was in corporate finance, and I enjoyed it. And that's it.[6]

Although he did not explicitly use the term, this MP clearly described the waiting line discussed above. Despite the fact that he was very interested in politics, he chose to avoid this long, codified wait. His political activity was "on the side"; he was a party member and the executive director of a political think tank for many years. This position allowed him to associate with MPs and have the feeling he was active in politics, without having the constraints or the position of subordination (as a staffer or a municipal councilor), or the professional instability that are all associated with political activity.

It would thus be misguided to believe that these MPs did not have an interest in politics. One other LREM MP, who was close to Emmanuel Macron even before he launched his campaign, said this very explicitly when he talked about "the beauty of the election":

So yeah, I always had that in the back of my mind, the idea of working for the public sector, but not necessarily as an MP. Given that for me, the idea of an election is the most amazing thing. Democratic legitimacy is wonderful ... at the time I was preparing ENA as a kind of trampoline, but for all the wrong reasons. It was to be propelled into the upper echelons of French administration, you know. But life took me elsewhere. When Macron was elected, I had the choice of working as an advisor at the Elysée, but I chose election. That's what's important to me.[7]

When it comes to the disaffection for elected mandates among the social elites, we see that the decline in income, which is often given as an explanation, is at best one aspect of a more complex whole. Worse, this aspect was essentially invalidated by the 2017 election, which saw the return en masse of these social elites who had disappeared from the Bourbon Palace. Table 5.1 below shows the evolution of the social make-up of the Assembly, including for 2017.[8] As per usual, managers are significantly overrepresented, but more unusually, business owners and CEOs are too (Michon, 2019). As for the level of study, 2017 saw a significant increase in the proportion of highly educated MPs—without, however, reaching the level of the golden age of French technocracy of the 1970s. In 2017, 30% of MPs had a masters degree (compared to 21% in 2017) and 10% had a PhD (unchanged). If we look only at those who graduated from the prestigious *grandes écoles* or ENA (but not including Sciences Pos, which have a specific status) the increase is more than 50% compared to the previous legislature. In 2017, the Assembly was bourgeois, and probably the most socially homogeneous it has been in the last half-century. The traditional gap between the population that is elected and the population that is represented increased after this election.

As should be clear by now, the social elites deserted politics not so much because they refused to engage, but because they refused to engage *on the terms* imposed by a political world governed by waiting. The waiting line they faced was highly dissuasive, especially for people who had viable and stimulating alternatives.

Exploring the Political *Illusio*

In spite of the difficulties laid out in the previous chapter, and in spite of the drop in remuneration at the National Assembly, there is still no shortage of candidates for these positions in France, nor has there been any shortage in recent years. Of course, the profile of these candidates may vary. In recent decades the social elites who used to dominate the lower house have progressively given way to members of the upper middle classes, up until 2017, when the former made somewhat of a return. But once they set out on this path, many of them then want to remain active in politics. So what is it they get from this activity that they cannot find elsewhere, if it isn't the pay or the prestige?

To answer this question, we have to move away from the novices and talk to MPs who have been present in the political field for a long time. Alongside the study of political newcomers, or just after it, I conducted a number of interviews, sometimes meeting with them several times, with politicians who have spent decades in politics and who had also held positions in the executive branch. I conducted interviews with one former president, two former prime ministers, and two former ministers—all of whom had also been MPs at some stage.

From this immersion in the perspective of people who dedicated their lives to politics, we can see that politics provides something "that no other activity could" (in the words of the former president), that other activities "seem very bland" by comparison (former MP). Moreover, these interviewees all declare that they are "passionate" about politics. It is, in the words of a former Prime Minister, a "passion" he worked hard to keep under control, always being at the risk of it tipping over into "addiction"—a term that I heard more than once. In other words, they recognize that politics has a particular value and intensity that they could find nowhere else. Or, in the words of Pierre Bourdieu, they shared the same *illusio*, a belief in the superiority and particular importance of the stakes in this particular space, one that is not visible to outsiders.

The next few pages explore their representations of politics, and as such constitute elements towards the analysis of the political *illusio*. One clarification may be useful, however. First, studying *illusio* within a group does not mean that we will be looking for the causes of these actors' commitments. Not only may these actors sometimes only have a limited awareness of what pushes them into action, but such motivations may vary from one person to another. But I believe it is a good starting point to better grasp what is otherwise described in pop-psychological terms, or pathologized. Second, exploring the make-up of this *illusio* does not mean that the people in question are deluded, or that they are lying to themselves about the reality of their practice. It is simply an attempt to reconstitute their mental cosmogony, to make sense of their worldview, and thus get a sense of what makes politics attractive to them and what makes them dedicate all their time and energy to it.

The Power to Do and the Right to Represent

When we ask MPs about what seems essential to them in politics, it is the "power to act" that is most often emphasized. A former prime minister said as much when asked about what he values in politics, responding without hesitation "being in the driving seat." He did acknowledge difficulties, however, and recognized that his action was not unconstrained. In spite of the fact that there are more failed initiatives than successful ones, he confirmed what seems to be an iron law of political action, this power to act is uniformly hailed as an important source of motivation.

If you listen to seasoned politicians, they will tell you that power is never valued in itself, but rather for what it enables them to do, on a large scale. The commonly defended idea is that politics is the only place where it is possible to profoundly and extensively change citizens' lives. The interview conducted with the former president makes this explicit.

> Politics brings what no other activity can, the idea—accurate or not—of being able to change peoples' lives. That's it. You may be successful in a business career or in your intellectual life. But you won't have the feeling of changing peoples' lives. In politics that is immediately tangible. Is true in local level positions. A town can be transformed by a mayor. And at the national level if the law is passed and you are responsible for it, then . . . .

He then, somewhat emphatically, concurred that "politics brings what no other human activity can, the right, and even the responsibility to change the lives of others. That is why it is such a strong motivation."

The same argument was expressed by a former minister, who had previously worked as a doctor, who said that "it is marvelous, people can't understand. If you're a professor of medicine, you can't change everything for the next twenty years—unless you're doing fundamental research. It is the same if I am a doctor: I have patients I look after, I have a practice I look after. . . . But as a politician you can decide tomorrow that you will introduce Social Security. You implement that policy and all at once you've transformed the lives of millions of people, for decades to come. There aren't many jobs where you can do that. Even Bernard Arnault [France's richest person and CEO of the global company LVMH] can't do that. So, it's fascinating. You change peoples' lives, over the long term."

Looking at these two statements alongside each other shows that one of the clear stated foundations of political engagement is this impact on collective life, which they consider incomparable. And although his example is different, a former minister for foreign affairs I interviewed essentially expressed the same idea when he argued that what separates politics from other activities is the ability to "wage war." He concluded, "you can drive a country to war, or bring about peace. It is dizzying."

Power is clearly one of the pillars of this political *illusio*, as described by political leaders. In their words, is not an empty power, or power-for-power's sake, but a power that can make concrete changes, laws, transformative measures. Looking at this aspect allows us to understand what motivates MPs to remain in power, sometimes against all odds. Taking into account this aspect is also essential because it explains why, by their own admission, most of their time is dedicated to much less noble activities—whether the constant creation of coalitions, desperate power grabbing, or as one of the interviewees said, "spending the day plotting."

But there is another trait that constantly comes back in the comments of these experienced politicians, and it has to do with representation. They value this part of their role, which has been the heart of modern democracy for the last 200 years. The individuals interviewed here all spontaneously emphasized the importance of this aspect of their work, which leads them to speak "in the name of others."

A product of the act of political delegation, representation happens on all levels, from the lowest administrative level to the highest, from the local scene to the international stage. The former president mentioned, in two successive sentences, the fact that he was "representing France overseas" but also that he was being present in "little village ceremonies, with drums and trumpets." According to him, the local stakes were even higher because the presence of the elected representative embodies this fuzzy entity that is the nation, and "brings the Republic to life," acting as "the key element in social and national cohesion." When questioned about what they lost at the end of the mandate, the same person continued, not without a certain sense of humor, "what you lose is the idea of representation. When you're president, you represent the nation. When you're mayor, you represent the town. When you're a former president, what do you represent? The past. That's something different. You no longer have that mission, that function."

This belief in the importance of representation is also a character trait that separates newer MPs from those who have more experience. As we saw in the previous chapter, novices are reluctant to attend the numerous ceremonies associated with their political activity. They talk about such events in pejorative terms, complaining about "the retirement home bingo" for example, and say they are "wasting their time" in these "unending" duties. This is not the case for more experienced MPs who consider such activities in a very positive light. The former president, who was an MP for a long time, talks about the pleasure he takes in such collective ceremonies. According to him, "there is pleasure to be taken in meetings," or again: "Politics is not a solitary pleasure." This remains true in the face of difficult interactions, which are seen as being an integral part of their activity—not only as a way of collecting information but also of showing they are listening to people's troubles. Through their presence, constituents can see what these MPs represent, can see them taking into account the needs and demands those who voted them in.

This idea of representation, of embodying an entity that is bigger than oneself, is theoretically made possible by the delegation that happens through the vote. In practice, it is made real by a series of actions—from the constant naming and the use of titles (*Monsieur le Président*, "Mister President," a formulation that is used for all other elected positions), to the ordinary everyday privileges—the motorcade, the attention, the presents. This repeated servile behavior ends up producing a belief in the reality of this act of transubstantiation that turns the physical person into a moral entity. One former mayor of a major city explicitly recounts how everything in his everyday life reiterated his special status, "While you're doing that [politics], your secretary looks after your taxes, your chauffeur drives your car, your motor convoy means you don't have to stop at red lights. If there are any traffic jams you have a siren so you can get through. You don't ask for any of that, but it just happens. And if you are a bit late at the airport you go via the special room, and you board the plan just three minutes before it takes off."

These innumerable signs constantly remind politicians of their special status on an everyday basis, which means they give in to a specific personality and certain traits that political psychologists have described as "egotistical" or "narcissistic." It is for the same reason that the discourse on the "gift of the self," and its twin, the idea of "vocation," are so frequently heard in the mouths of these politicians. As a result of the extensive demands made of them, the fact that their schedule is constrained and partly out of their hands, politicians have the impression of not being fully in control of their lives. They are also aware—or if they want to avoid deep depression they must quickly realize—that the attacks that they regularly receive are directed against their role rather than them as individuals, that such attacks are targeted more at what they represent than who they are.

High-Intensity Life

These explanations of what is specific to political engagement would remain quite abstract if it were not for another aspect that is also regularly mentioned by long-term MPs, which is the intensity of political life. Although it is much more concrete, this aspect is also regularly cited as being an addictive part of the political world. Whether to explain how exhausting a life spent in politics is, or to explain how much they miss this rhythm at the end of their mandate, the MPs emphasize this permanent stress. One MP describes politics as "a universe in which everything is catalyzed, feelings, hatred, love, everything is more intense. Everything is amplified and exacerbated."[9]

This intensity is particularly pronounced during the campaign periods. The various books, journalistic investigations, or documentaries focusing on the campaign trail stress the rhythm of these democratic processes in which the pursuit of power seems to go hand in hand with a life of excess which seems to justify everything. Some have even made this the backbone of their narrative, such as the American journalist Hunter S. Thompson. In his now classic *Fear and Loathing on the Campaign Trail '72*, the author describes the unsuccessful Democrats' campaign against Nixon. The book brings together the chronicles the author published in *Rolling Stone* over the course of this campaign year, and it leaves nothing out. The permanent tension, excessive alcohol, and even drug use are described at length. Never having learned the codes of the journalistic establishment in Washington, Thompson does not censor his prose: the reader is made aware of everything that happened on his watch, and of all that he himself experienced. The lack of sleep, the constant moving, which leads candidates to "spend more time with journalists than with their own wives," as well as the unexpected events that influence everyday life, all accurately reflect this very specific rhythm of politics. The studies in social sciences that have focused on this say the same thing. In his account of a local electoral campaign studied through participant observation, the sociologist Matthew Mahler tells of how he eventually accepted that he would not sleep more than a few hours a night for several months, while immersed in the rhythm of the collective organization he was part of (Mahler, 2011, p. 153).

This intensity is well known to observers of the political world. From TV series to novels, it has been a key element in the description of this milieu. And it does not just concern election campaigns. This intensity is due to something that is much less frequently mentioned, the infinite nature of politics, at least as far as politicians feel they must practice it. What makes this an endless quest is that the latter are constantly looking for new people to convince. Whether potential voters, or supporters who will back them in their ventures, MPs recount how they must constantly be on the lookout for new sources of support and meet new people, wherever possible.

Thus, this former minister adds that more than the long working hours, it was the lack of a potential end, of a limit to the working day, that is characteristic of his life as an MP. "In terms of working hours, I would say that being a politician is as intense as being a doctor in intensive care. Even in terms of stress. The difference is that when you are a doctor, after your shift is over, you go to bed. Sometimes you might go overtime but if there's no one there you go home. In politics, it is never over. You might do 12 or 14 or 15 meetings in the day and at the end of the last one, your chauffeur says, 'yes but you haven't been to see the majorettes, it's 40 kilometers away, do you want to go?' And you say yes. Because there are always more voters to see."

Because they must try and convert an ever-greater number of people to their cause, political leaders are engaged in a competition that is paradoxically endless, but which can also end at any time. A minister can lose his job from one day to the next. And although the president or MPs can only be dismissed in rare cases, their employment contract is nevertheless for a limited time only, which forces them to try and constantly make themselves visible in the public space—or at least they think it does. They may therefore spend their days trying to avoid derailment while rushing around at breakneck speed. This was the impression one MP gave when talking about his days as a minister and head of his party, "When you're on a breakfast show at 8:00 o'clock in the morning, under the lights for 10 minutes, then you go to the National Assembly for question time, then in the evening you speak at a meeting in front of 4,000 people . . . it's a bit like a roller coaster. Everybody is licking your boots, but you have also been the subject of scathing criticism in a newspaper, and you don't know why. Add to this the fact that the *Canard Enchaîné* [a satirical weekly famous for unearthing political scandals] may have revealed your mother-in-law didn't pay her taxes three years ago . . . you see, bombs are constantly raining down."

It is therefore not surprising that the same person, a former medical doctor, declares that politics is the activity that generates the most endorphins, the hormones secreted by the brain to minimize feelings of pain. According to the scientists that study them, they also have euphoric properties close to those of opiates. Other MPs were less opaque, describing politics as a hard drug. One MP, for example, congratulated himself on not "having got addicted," not having "developed the politician's illness." Another, interviewed by Alizée Delpierre as part of a study on MPs' attitude toward the media, protested that he was not "addicted to the media." But he nevertheless recognizes that "when you start to get used to it, start seeing yourself on the screen, hearing yourself on the radio—because it does flatter the ego a bit in spite of everything—and well, you have to know that it can end any day, it's not stable, it can also fall apart. And then afterward, it makes you sick, you can't get over it, it's like a wound, a narcissistic wound perhaps" (Delpierre, 2015, p.79). It is when an all-encompassing activity, a total social fact, comes to an end that its nature become clear. Most MPs interviewed mentioned the feeling of emptiness that took hold of them once their position came to an end, sometimes suddenly. Although many use the word, few accepted to go into details on this feeling, or to talk about depression, even though they say that they had seen it in their colleagues who had been through the same situation.

That is why this interview extract with the former minister—who had on several occasions thought he would be made prime minister, and who even implied that he had seriously considered running for president—is both rich and very rare. This testimony seems to corroborate the image of elected representatives who are disconnected from the lives of citizens, and such comments will likely spark either irritation or amusement from readers, and maybe both. But above all the interview describes the environment in which these high-profile politicians live, and in so doing reveals the material and symbolic foundations that allow this disconnect to occur, and enables them to develop the *illusio* that is so specific to professional politics. The extract below has only been amended to preserve the anonymity of the person and has been slightly condensed:

So, when everything stops, you no longer do these grand things you have dedicated your life to doing. No one asks you your opinion on important questions anymore. You're not in your Ministry, instead you're in your 80m2 apartment. And you have to pay the rent. You have to go to [the town where he was Mayor], and you have to take Air France [instead of an official diplomatic plane]. But you don't even know how to take an Air France ticket!
Really?
Of course! You've been mayor for 25 years, MP, minister, and you don't know. You wonder what card number you have to put in, what program, and you don't know. So, you ask your former secretary, who is now the new minister's secretary. And she can't answer your phone call because she doesn't have time.
So, everything in your day brings you down. And there's nobody around to praise you [he had just finished describing how the entourage around MPs was both dangerous and essential for maintaining belief in one's worth].
What is more, you are not part of any circles, of any clans vying for power. Because all your friends have become ministers and you're the only

one who didn't. You turn on the television and you see your friends all the time, on 24/7 news channels.

And that is when you have to face the facts; you have become a spectator. It's like having been an actor in the theater all of one's life, but then when you don't get the part you still go to the theater anyway to see the show. It is extremely depressing. You have to live with it and accept the loss of power.

* * *

Why do people get, and stay, into politics? And why, once they have reached a certain level of responsibility, do politicians try to stay there? Although it does not provide a full answer to this question, this chapter offers elements of a response. First in terms of what it is not, showing that common explanations are not as relevant as they are (widely) assumed to be. For example, based on the French case we have seen that money is probably not the primary motivation for politicians—although it is often assumed to be. Although remuneration is substantial at the national level, and for some is an increase compared to what would have been paid before, for most MPs these salaries are not so different from what they would have been paid in the private sector. Furthermore, when considered in terms of the number of hours they work, this remuneration is not that attractive. The argument is similar if we look at prestige. In France at least—but this is also true in many other countries—politics is not particularly prestigious, on the contrary. Worse still, the numerous acts of violence that MPs have been subject to in recent years in different countries shows that apathy is becoming closer to hatred, which does not lend support to this interpretation.

So why do politicians persist in this ill-reputed occupation? Although it only partially sheds lights on political engagement, this exploration of the political *illusio* provides important elements to understand what drives MPs. The feeling of "changing peoples' lives," the right to be speak on behalf of a higher entity and represent the nation, or the high-intensity high-stress life, these are three elements that are often mentioned in the interviews. For long-term politicians, these aspects compensate for what is sometimes seen as a sacrifice, in terms of private life, working hours, and other difficulties. Other studies will have to pursue the causes of political engagement more deeply, along with politicians' worldviews and the differences that may exist—between them, between eras, and between political systems.

This result in turn casts doubt on a common trope, one regularly floated some, who propose higher revenues—sometimes in exchange for a lower number of MPs—as a solution to the "crisis of democracy." The idea is not that MPs are badly paid in themselves. With €5,500 net per month, they are still in the top 3% of the population in terms of earnings. Instead, the logic is that higher remuneration (associated with a decline in the number of parliamentarians) would help to attract better, more "skilled" candidates for these mandates. The argument is that MPs, like any worker, will only apply for a job if the advantages outweigh the disadvantages. If their "minimum reservation wage" is too high for what they consider to be the cost of the mandate, then they will not apply.

The evidence presented in this chapter calls into question the idea that increased pay would lead to a different demographic make-up of the political field, and to a better functioning political world. In spite of its somewhat negative image, politics still continues to attract countless candidates, regardless of money. Much more important seems to be the question of the time that must be spent waiting, often in uncertain positions, in order to access the national political level. The waiting line that built up before 2017 to access national positions was more dissuasive to members of the upper classes than working conditions or pay.

If the goal is to diversify recruitment or attract more competent candidates, paying MPs more would therefore only have a limited effect. But this is not the only, or even the most important problem, with this proposal. The argument of remuneration—which is not reflected in the facts—is based on the hypothesis that social status or education is a good indicator of skill and ability. Yet this relationship is at best unclear. One recent study on the recruitment of teachers shows that higher education does not necessarily lead to successful pedagogy.[10] Others examples could be mentioned, but in the case of politicians, the connection is even less straightforward. Are academic success and social status good indicators of someone's ability to contribute to the legislative process, control the government, or represent the nation? This logic, if pushed to the extreme, would lead to a National Assembly made up exclusively of graduates from prestigious universities, senior civil servants, or Fortune 500 CEOs—or whatever other sign of excellence might be relevant at a particular moment. The theory of representation that underlies these arguments is a theory that seems to overlook the very idea of representation itself, or which defends a highly elitist version of it.

CONCLUSION

IN THE WAITING LINE

In 2017, a shift occurred. A large number of candidates with what would otherwise be unusual trajectories landed in national politics. We can learn some lessons from this unusual experience. The most obvious one is that the promise of political renewal was not kept. Of course, the 2017 election modified the rules for accessing the political field—at least for that one time. But what was its real impact? The promise, widespread during the campaign, was that political novices would breathe new life into the "stinking swamp" of politics, that they would be vectors of a profound renewal. The results presented in the different chapters of this book show that this change was limited, however. Genuine novices only very rarely managed to carve out a place for themselves. In the three first years of the mandate, they were restricted to a limited role and rarely were able to access prominent positions.

Conversely, other MPs who arrived at the Assembly during the June 2017 intake were able to take the reins rapidly. They requested, and were granted, frontline positions. They successfully proposed bills and important proposals, sometimes on several occasions. They managed to stand out from the crowd of more than 300 MPs elected for La République en Marche in 2017. But although they passed for novices in the confusion surrounding the elections, few of them genuinely were. On the contrary, most of them had in fact followed the same golden path that Emmanuel Macron had denounced during the campaign. They were former campaign staffers, parliamentary assistants, or cabinet members, and much like the new head of state, were able to make the most of the situation.

This book has explored the reasons for this stability, in spite of the significant upheaval of 2017. Although the faces changed, the rules of the political game remained the same. Knowledge acquired in previous positions was still useful, as was the social capital that could be accumulated there, be it connections with journalists, frontline political leaders, or senior public servants. These former members of the inner political circles even benefited

The Candidates. Étienne Ollion, Oxford University Press. © Oxford University Press 2024.
DOI: 10.1093/oso/9780197665954.003.0007

from the presence of these novices who were unfamiliar with the mores of political life. Under normal circumstances, they would have had to compete against all the other members of the parliamentary group, but in this case, competition was less intense because around a third of the majority group was unfamiliar with the rules. This contributed to the progression of those who had more experience within the party hierarchy.

The consequence was that traditional logics were perpetuated, but also that the parliament lost some of its power in relation to the executive. The balance of powers, which under the Fifth Republic already favored the executive, was further accentuated. Faced with colleagues who had little experience, it was easier for the government to get its bills passed without established opposition or counterpowers. Moreover, given that these MPs owed their election to the president of Republic, it resulted in even greater loyalty from the former. At the very most some dropped out, most often alone or in small groups, without ever endangering the parliamentary majority.

Finally, as though moved by the cunning of executive reason, these novices were ultimately the best possible guarantee for a political system that was not reformed in the least. They were, following Lampedusa's oft-cited maxim, actively but unwittingly involved in ensuring that "everything changes so that nothing changes." How could it be otherwise? In the epilogue, we return to this question and to the fate of the 2017 novices a few years later. Before that however, we have to draw some conclusions, and tie together some of the theoretical threads we have spun around the question of the waiting line.

The Politics of Waiting Lines

A study of a specific political experiment, this book has also sought to draw attention to the peculiar social arrangement that waiting lines are. As we have already mentioned, these lines have three main characteristics: they socialize, they select, and they individualize.

It is easy enough to see how the waiting line socializes. Waiting your turn in a space where you hope to progress helps you to internalize the norms of that environment. Over time candidates adopt the values of the space they want to integrate and come to value them. They progressively acquire the knowledge and skills that allow them to operate efficiently in this space. The novices' feeling of being maladroit and inexpert when they arrived in the National Assembly in 2017 is proof of the importance of this socialization.

Up until then they were removed from national policy, and many expressed their incomprehension about the functioning of the institution. They were surprised, sometimes audibly so, about the demands of their positions—for example about the specific pace of work. Because they had not been trained in the rules of parliamentary procedure or the ways of this highly codified institution, they necessarily committed a certain number of blunders, which more experienced actors in the political field did not fail to ridicule.

However, it is important to go beyond this superficial perspective to see the full socializing role of the waiting line. Indeed, the latter also inculcates a sense of limits to those who wait. Candidates must adapt their practices to those of their colleagues and patrons. They also internalize, and in so doing accept, the succession of stages they must pass through before accessing the positions they covert. They push back when some seek to challenge the order of successions or of the line. The criticisms leveled at Emmanuel Macron during the 2017 campaign are the best example of this. Week after week, Macron was accused by his more experienced peers of "wanting to go too fast," of "skipping stages." Over the months of the campaign, this injunction to wait one's turn was repeated dozens of times, and it remains a good illustration of the moral economy that structures these social arrangements.

The waiting line also operates as a means of selection. If it had a physical form, and operated exclusively according to the principle of waiting, progression along the line would be clear and straightforward. But most waiting lines in our society do not have this clear material reality. They allow for a certain flexibility in the attribution of positions. Whether because there are in fact several lines (one for VIPs, and one for others, as in airports, for example), or because the space in itself is segregated (public and private hospitals, for example), there are certain characteristics or circumstances that enable a more rapid passage through the line. The more metaphorical waiting lines operate as a sorting mechanism, according to several factors. Someone might be excluded from the line because another candidate is preferred, one who is more highly educated, wealthier, or more docile perhaps. They may also self-exclude, particularly those with the least resources who cannot afford to wait. This might be one reason for the disappearance of working-class politicians from national politics; they end up leaving when they realized they would never be given a chance to run. But this might also be the reason for the less visible yet equally clear withdrawal of the elites from the national political scene. These elites have turned away from politics over the last 20 years because of the long waiting times—sometimes many years—that they would have had to spend in positions that were less prestigious, less well paid, and more unstable than those they could access (more rapidly) in the private sector. In other words, because they had other options, these elites chose a different career path. Yet they returned to parliament in 2017, exactly at the moment when it became clear the waiting line could be avoided.

Finally, the waiting line individualizes. This simply means that where there is waiting, there is scarcity; there are many more candidates than there are positions available. The existence of this political reserve army, to paraphrase Marx, is not without consequences. In this situation of a latent war of many against many, collective strategies are always likely to be ephemeral. Alliances are temporary and focused on obtaining an intermediary goal. Attacks may be brutal because what matters is accessing the next level. Because they are in constant competition, those in the waiting line develop an anxiety that prevents them adopting collective strategies. This is all the more true because any attempt at collective organizing may lead to the loss of past investments. In other words, people lining up experience the same "serial existence" analyzed by Sartre in his *Critique of the Dialectical Reason* (1976 [1960]). To illustrate this notion, Sartre used the metaphor of people who are waiting for a packed bus. All of them know that when it arrives it will be full, and that they will have to fight to get on. But because they are focused on this immediate and individual course of action, they neglect alternative options—for instance collectively organizing to demand more buses. In these circumstances, where individual salvation seems possible if the individual plays their own cards right, individual interests dominate over collective logics.

Waiting Lines Everywhere

Before the COVID pandemic brought them back all around the world, with queues outside shops and testing centers, these waiting lines had become less visible in public space. In rich countries they were even considered a sad throwback to the past, or something reserved for developing nations. Didn't American propaganda against the USSR focus specifically on its waiting lines? In our collective minds, they were something that disproportionately affected the poorest in a given society.

Yet they hadn't disappeared altogether. Some physical lines still existed: to take trains, to access public services, or pay for goods. It was simply that some of them had become less visible. Techniques for managing clientele, aimed at euphemizing waiting, had made them more discreet. Digital technology had furthered this process by allowing this waiting to be dematerialized. But waiting was, and is no less present, whether on the telephone, or when trying to make appointments on the Internet, the experience of the waiting line is ubiquitous, in powerful but invisible forms.

Politics is therefore not the only area where this phenomenon operates, far from it. There are numerous examples of professions where an order of succession is standard. Accessing a position in academia is an example of this. The drop in the number of available positions over recent decades has created a situation of rarity. Candidates in this sector often have to wait several years after defending their PhD thesis to obtain a position, and while they wait they alternate between postdoctoral work, short-term contracts, or unemployment. In 2020, the average age at which early career lecturers (*maître de conference*, the first grade in the profession in France) were hired was 34 years old, a figure that has since increased. It is difficult to not see this system as a waiting line in which candidates apply for rarefied positions with unequal chances. In situations that are often financially difficult and always unstable, candidates for these academic positions try to publish, and to acquire experience before the next round of recruitment. Waiting lines favor those with resources and we can assume the uncertainty they provoke is not conducive to quality research. Contrary to the idea that competition is a positive force for innovation, one could easily show that in addition to affecting the well-being of the candidates, the ensuing anxiety and pressure to publish probably lead to intellectual conformism.[1]

Many other sectors are at least partially organized around this principle. The world of journalism is another example. In this area, before accessing a permanent contract, candidates have to conduct as many internships and work placements as possible, sometimes for years. Although there are exceptions, with a happy few hired immediately after journalism school, hundreds of others wait in a line that has no centralized organization, but is not without hierarchy, before getting a contract. In the public radio service in France, this situation is institutionalized through a specific system. Young people who graduate from journalism school, and who occasionally work for one of the radio stations may eventually apply to get on a specific list called "*le planning*." This is highly competitive. The written application is followed by an oral presentation in front of industry professionals, and the candidates can only apply like this twice in their career. If they are selected, they are offered a six-year contract, during which they may—if their work is deemed satisfactory—eventually gain a permanent position. During these years, they will replace colleagues in local radio stations, change subjects as often as they change offices, and spend a lot of time in hotels. This experience is instructive, but it is very unstable—apprenticeship is also a permanent trial period.

The temp sector is yet another example of the waiting line logic. The ethnographer Sébastien Chauvin has shown how major temporary labor companies in Chicago asked those they employ to come into the central office each morning, sometimes for more than an hour, before being sent out on appointments. This was the case even though some of them have been working in the same company for years. The reason for asking them to come by the agency first is so that their motivation can be evaluated, they can be tested (obliging them to get up early), and to discipline them by reminding them every morning of their job insecurity.

Although ubiquitous, these waiting lines are not universal. There are entire sectors where the balance between supply and demand is reversed, and which are not concerned by this kind of management; for an example, I only have to look at my students, who are IT engineers and data scientists. At the moment, they are hired even before they graduate from university. More recently the pandemic has demonstrated strong demand for both social and health workers. In both cases formal qualifications or competitive exams are clearly necessary, but for those who pass these requirements there is almost no waiting period. There are also whole sectors in which there is no waiting because there is no possible progression. Shop assistants, checkout workers, and call center operators have very slim chances of accessing more senior positions, often held by men, or by someone with slightly higher qualifications. For a whole series of occupations, entry level positions are often the only ones available.

Although waiting lines are not everywhere, they are clearly one way of progressing in different kinds of contemporary spaces. Are there more lines than there used to be? We would need a specific historical study to be able to tell. But one thing is sure, the acceleration of time diagnosed by the German sociologist Harmut Rosa (2013 [2005]) is by no means a fluidification in which social inequality disappears. Even if we were to be able to demonstrate that an acceleration happened, this contemporary speed described by Rosa has not been to the benefit of all, as some people still wait and sometimes for a long time. Worse still, in a world where speed has become the norm, and in which waiting lines still exist, those who are asked to wait suffer twice. Their trajectory is slowed down, but it is also devalued, both in their eyes and for others.

This book has therefore tried to draw attention to these social forms that structure contemporary societies, and to the effects on the individuals they entangle. Other questions should also be raised. What are the different types of waiting lines? Are they explicitly presented as such or are they implicit? What are the main selection criteria on which they operate (is it duration, as in waiting for social housing; urgency, as in hospital triage; or something else entirely)? What are its effects on social organization as a whole? This raises numerous other questions, which may provide the basis for other studies, or sites for future research.[2]

The goal of this book has been to analytically dissect these social forms that govern practice and that contribute to the reproduction of the social order. Socialization shapes the individuals within these mechanisms, selection removes those who do not conform, and individualization limits the desires for radical strategies to pursue personal initiative. Given that these waiting lines are all the more conservative because they are not recognized as such, and because the organizing principle and consequences are never explicit, it is important bring them into the light and to try and show the type of individual produced by a society of candidates.

EPILOGUE

June 22, 2022. Exactly five years after they entered the world of politics under intense scrutiny from the French media, some of the novices from 2017 returned to the assembly for a second term. There were not as many of them as in 2017; some did not run again, and others did not make it through the gauntlet of the election. Yet they were more than might have been expected. Political observers, myself included, had depicted an adjustment to the political sphere that was so difficult few of us imagined that these amateurs, who arrived in politics almost by accident in 2017, would be desperate to stay for a second term. We were partly wrong; prediction is a difficult art in social sciences. In the end, among the novices from 2017, more than half wanted to return to the parliamentary benches for a second term. Between the socialization to political life acquired over the course of the previous five years, and a feeling that they would have a greater possibility for effective action the second time around, a substantial number decided to run again.

However, the 2022 legislature was different from the one they had known. Emmanuel Macron had lost his comfortable parliamentary majority. There were only 235 LREM (La République en Marche) MPs, down by more than 100 from 2017. The left had managed to save itself from anticipated electoral disaster with a last-minute alliance, forming the NUPES (New Popular, Environmental, and Social Union [Nouvelle Union Populaire, Écologique et Sociale]), which is now the largest opposition force, with 151 members. But the biggest surprise, and probably the biggest change, came from the other side of the chamber. The extreme-right party RN (Rassemblement National), led by Marine Le Pen, had triumphal success ,with no fewer than 89 MPs. Although the party (founded by her father Jean-Marie Le Pen in the 1970s) had been elected to parliament before, this was the first time they won so many seats. With a sixth of the total number of MPs, the RN is now fully a part of French political life; after conquering ideas, discourses, votes, they have now claimed seats in parliament—and the substantial public funding that goes with them.

The fate of this new legislature, different and less docile than that of 2017, will be left to future researchers. For the moment, let me just note that that under the three legislatures I have studied, democratic debate is suffering. The symptoms of this have taken different forms. Under François Hollande, it emerged in the form of an internal fracture within the Socialist Party over the government's policies—which dozens of his own MPs considered too right-wing, and not in line with campaign promises. The continuous protest by these dissident MPs over the course of the legislature was put down by threats and by the use of the tools of rationalized parliamentarianism, which allow the executive to override parliament, thus preventing debate and the introduction of amendments. Under the first Macron presidency, the novice MPs were pushed into the background; they did not immediately realize the role they had to play, and only later understood the limited power they had. In the current parliament, initial debates were rich in content, probably due to the unseen diversity between parties, but even more, due to the lack of a clear majority, which forced the government to take parliament into account like never before in recent years. Yet as soon as summer was over, when came the time to negotiate the budget, the old habits returned, and the government once again turned to tools that enable it to force its legislation through, whether the parliament wanted it or not. This change was tangible in the debates, and the tensions that arose in response to them. From a lively, sometimes chaotic atmosphere, the National Assembly went back to functioning according to its standard *modus operandi*, and democratic deliberation suffered as a result.

What this book, and its examples, demonstrate is that there is no point waiting for political life to change if there are simply casting changes (like in 2017), or renaming of political parties (as in 2022). If the goal is really to change politics, a claim that is often heard, it is clear that such measures are not sufficient, that other instruments must be mobilized. How can novices, people from outside the political field, but who have extensive life experience, contribute to the polis? Is it simply unreasonable to rapidly promote novices to positions of responsibility?

I do not believe so, and many experiences suggest that it is possible to have a legislature that is both competent and diverse in terms of their political experience. Examples abound. Ancient Greece provides us with a radical illustration of this problem, along with a solution. In this regime, where most positions were based on a random draw, and where the term was never longer than one or two years, the new arrivals knew nothing about the task they were asked to fulfill. But they were actively supported by people who knew about the work, but could not make any decisions, and who were hierarchically dependent on the selected politicians (Ismard, 2015). Although this democracy was highly imperfect, it provides a clue as to how inexperienced MPs may gain confidence in their initial steps.

One solution to the necessary incompetence of beginners lies in increased support from senior public servants, experienced staffers, or others. This is in fact what the various people working for them in parliament are supposed to do, whether as staffers or officials. But in France, these aides have been pared down to a strict minimum. Where an American senator has 30 to 40 staffers at their disposal, and German parliamentary groups are able to attract around 200 high-level collaborators (with the promise of attractive salaries), French MPs have three or four assistants. Democracy sometimes lies in these discrete material elements.

Beyond this, I believe we have to collectively free ourselves from certain expectations. Over the course of this study, I was struck by the prevalent mental image of what a "good politician" is, and how it affects the success of the said politicians. This is true for journalists, of course, whose way of dealing with politics is central because it can make and unmake careers. I have often overheard journalists in the Salle de Quatre Colonnes say that "the newbies are not up to scratch" (see Chapter 4). When I asked them what they meant by that, they came up with a list of expectations which ranged from "knowing how to talk" (by this, they meant talking like other politicians), or "being able to produce a political discourse" (having a clear position on a vast range of subjects). But aside from those who already have experience in politics, who has an opinion on a range of questions as diverse as green finance, secularism, voting methods, and France's trade policy? And who is naturally able to speak convincingly in front of a camera or take the microphone before the full chamber, under scrutiny from both cameras and more experienced colleagues, and talk for several minutes while members of the opposition do everything possible to upset you? Probably not very many people, unless they have been prepared for it.

One day in September 2015, I saw a new member of government arrive in the chamber. With his golden boy image, Emmanuel Macron had just been appointed minister for the economy and finance, after the surprise dismissal of his predecessor. In what must have been one of his first government question time sessions, I saw him stand up, begin to respond, and then progressively lose his composure. Even for those who are prepared, this is not an easy exercise, and the young minister—even though he was already well versed in politics—did not do very well. It is true that in addition to the reaction of the opposition, who were determined to stand up to him, he had made a mistake. In his hand, he held a long piece of paper, that accentuated his trembling hands as the yelling from the right of the chamber intensified. Eventually the minister cut his reply short and went and sat down, shamefaced, on the ministers' bench. "Beginner's mistake," commented my neighbor in the press gallery, who had seen many others. Macron would not make the same mistake again; he rapidly absorbed his media training, in which you learn not to look at the opposition if they are too intimidating, and to use small flashcards for notes, which are more discreet in more ways than one.

This example raises the question of what role journalists played in the lack of visibility of the 2017 novices. It seems clear that they were judging these new arrivals based on what they expected from the old ones, in terms of ethos, practice, and attitudes toward politics. This question of expectations goes beyond journalists, or even those who gravitate around MPs; citizens also make their own demands. During the first months of the 2017 legislature, there were many "ordinary citizens" who ridiculed the novices' "blunders," their discomfort, and made fun of them on social media. The demands of constant presence (in Paris, in the constituency), long hours (an MP can be called on at any time), the idea that a representative must be able to accept both virulent protests and minor aggressions on an everyday basis, show that there are many who have a specific image of what a politicians should be. But who would really consider this a desirable life? If the goal is that ordinary men and women get involved in politics, we must also stop expecting them to already possess the skills and practices, and stress-management techniques, that can only be acquired after extensive training. Failing that, professional politics will continue to be populated by people who have learned to deal with these situations by force of habit.

Much more is needed to restore a living democracy, in which many have lost faith. We only need look at the staggering decline in participation and high levels of electoral volatility both in France and overseas in recent decades, to see this. All these elements suggest the need for urgent and in-depth reflection on the way we do politics, the way we involve citizens, and the way we legitimate public decision-making. In their 2004 book, James S. Fishkin and Bruce Ackerman defend the idea of a *Deliberation Day*, a day dedicated to democracy, and more specifically to its debates. The authors call for this to be a public holiday, a day when everyone would stop working to discuss the life of the polis. Although the practical application appears complicated, and we clearly need more than one day to debate various social problems, this may be an idea worth considering. In fact, it may be time for our society to pause and to take the time to deliberate the rules that govern our collective political existence. Such a moment may well be our last chance to positively reshape our old institutions.

ACKNOWLEDGMENTS

Andrew Abbott, Catherine Achin, Camille Auzéby, Marie Bergström, Julien Boelaert, Éric Buge, Emmanuel Cayre, Maxime Chabriel, Yacine Chitour, Thomas Collas, Muriel Darmon, Karim Fertikh, Michaël Foessel, Marion Fourcade, Julie Fournier, Bertrand Garbinti, Daniel Gaxie, Mathieu Hauchecorne, Monique Labrune, Marine de Lassalle, Frédéric Lebaron, Wilfried Lignier, Corinne Luquiens, Hélène Michel, Sébastien Michon, Ragnhilde Muriaas, Michel Offerlé, and Frédéric Sawicki. Special thanks to Katharine Throssell, who brilliantly translated this text into English.

I am also very grateful to those who shared their stories and experiences with me in the interviews conducted for this research, and who will remained unnamed.

NOTES

Introduction

1. The party was renamed La République en Marche (The Republic on the Move) right after the elections. In the following manuscript, En marche! thus refers to the party before June 2017, and uses La République en Marche (LREM) after.
2. Email sent to potential donors, quoted by Le Point, May 12, 2016.
3. In so doing he reactivated a classic though cyclical trope in US politics (and beyond) against career politicians. In his landmark 1990 essay on amateurs in Congress, D. Canon wrote, "The suspicions held by many Americans of career politicians and the long-standing tradition of 'running against Washington' can be exploited by amateurs who can credibly claim that they are not 'one of them'" (Canon, 1990, p. 3).
4. See for instance Mansbridge (1999), Phillips (1995), Campbell et al. (2010), or Carnes (2012).
5. In this rich literature, see for instance Best and Cotta (2000); Matthews (1984), Norris and Lovenduski (1995), and, more recently, Ohmura et al. (2018) for a rich approach.
6. The list is long here too. Important literature looks at roll calls (Rice, 1927; Hix & Noury, 2007); surgery and constituency work (Fenno, 2003; Costa & Poyet, 2016); and the "roles" MPs define for themselves (Searing, 1994).
7. As the courts would decide later, it was his wife who had "no occupation," although she had been paid to work as a staffer for over two decades, receiving nearly 1 million euros of taxpayers' money for nonexistent work.
8. See N. Allen et al. (2020) for a recent overview, Michon and Ollion (2018) for a detailed analysis on the French case.
9. Of course, not all politicians want to become MPs and not all MPs want to become cabinet members. This is only a partial limitation to the waiting-line metaphor, as the modal situation is in fact this desire to move up the ladder following this established path. As we shall see, because the waiting line socializes, it produces desires among those who are in it.
10. There is a well-developed literature on the subject of waiting lines in the ex-USSR. Among the many texts, see the partially autobiographical work by Lidiya Ginzburg, on the siege of Leningrad during the winter of 1941 (1995). Another, very different literature that is particularly rich and sometimes useful on this subject lies at the intersection of different specializations—economics, organizations theory, and the interdisciplinary subfield of operations research. When applied, it aims to promote the best ways of having people wait (see, e.g., Hassin & Haviv, 2003).

Chapter 1

1. Michèle Delaunay, "Le tunnel, ou comment faire carrière sans mettre un pied dans la vraie vie," September 13, 2014, https://tinyurl.com/y6cehmav (accessed August 19, 2022).
2. According to my calculations, in the newspaper *Le Monde*, the average frequency of these terms was multiplied by 3 between 2010 and 2016 (before the beginning of Macron's campaign).
3. "We have all become so professional. . . . We know the answers to all the questions because we check them off with the journalists. The polls dictate our policies [. . .] All this [our career] decides our action" (translated from Danish, Season 1, episode 1, 2010).
4. Between 1986 and 2021, 28% of cabinet members in France were alumni from Sciences Po Paris, and 16% from ENA.
5. "The leadership of a state or of a party by men who (in the economic sense of the word) live exclusively for politics and not off politics means necessarily a 'plutocratic' recruitment of the leading political strata" (Weber, [1919] 1946, p. 86).
6. See, for instance, the book by two journalists, who use this term in their title: Michaela Möller, Anders Rydell, *Broilers: Den nya makthavarna och det samhälle som formade dem* (Norstedts, 2014).
7. UKIP leader Nigel Farage did his best to always look "un-politician." He took regular jabs at the "Westminster Bubble," and he apparently insisted on conducting interviews in a pub (Hardman, 2018, p. 210).
8. Marine Le Pen "attempted a Macronian maneuver," and ran the risk of failure, according to Lorrain de Saint Affrique," in *France-Soir*, September 3, 2016.
9. Interview with a Socialist MP, March 2015.
10. Quoted in Boelaert et al. (2017, p. 78).
11. Although in Bourdieusian analysis the autonomization of fields is often seen in a positive light as it grants more power to specialists, one can wonder if this would be the case for the political field, since it increases the separation between the public and its representatives. This, in turn, sheds lights on the dual nature of the autonomization of fields: it ensures less encroachment from other social forces—first the economy—but it also excludes laypeople from participating in its activities.
12. And to a certain extent fame (Canon, 2011).
13. David Amiel and Ismael Emelien, *Le progrès ne tombe pas du ciel: Un manifeste* (Fayard, 2019).
14. This could be translated as "get-outism," from the French *dégager*, which means to get rid of something.
15. Quoted in Martigny (2017, p. 50).
16. Interview with Emmanuel Macron, *Journal du dimanche*, February 12, 2017, quoted in Strudel (2017, p. 209).
17. "Appelez-moi populiste si vous voulez," *Journal du dimanche*, March 18, 2017.
18. This is all the more true because the funding regulations forbid extremely large donations, imposing a limit of 7,500€ per person per year for individual contributions.

This rule, which has been in place since the 1990s, is designed to avert the intrusion of economic interests into the election and prevent the direct conversion of economic capital into political capital.
19. RTL, December 1, 2016.
20. Political scientist Raphaël Cos and his colleagues counted 380 propositions, compared to 162 for Sarkozy in 2012 and 264 for Hollande in 2012 (Cos, 2019).
21. Recalling once again the well-known adage that it takes a lot of capital to make a revolution.

Chapter 2

1. Campaign film from La République en Marche for the legislative elections.
2. See, for instance, Boelaert et al. (2017).
3. Data from François and Grossman (2011, pp. 364–380).
4. Interview with a party member, March 2018.
5. Interview with a party member, March 2018.
6. Interview with a party member, March 2018.
7. For a recent overview, see Allen et al. (2020). See Michon and Ollion (2018) on the French case.
8. But see the analysis of the careers of MPs in Germany (Ohmura et al., 2017), in the Netherlands (Turner-Zwinkels & Mills, 2020), or the analysis of the trajectories of senior civil servants in France (Bellon et al., 2018).
9. The years before this 20th birthday were not taken into account in calculating distances. In the case of MPs who were in several positions, rules were established in order to code states. A national-level position took precedence over a local mandate, and a local mandate over work as a collaborator (except for municipal councilors who were also collaborators, who were coded as the latter because that was probably more lucrative than the indemnity they received for their local mandate).
10. As Thomas Collas notes in his chapter, it avoids the problem of sensitivity and synchronicity that other models may encounter. Hamming distances, used for instance by Lesnard (2008), are very sensitive to this synchronicity: what happens in one year is compared to what happens in other sequences that same year. Multiphase analysis also focuses on synchronicity, which in cases like MPs with their staggered elections is central, but it does so phase by phase.
11. The dissimilarity calculations were completed using an optimal matching algorithm for each phase, with a substitution intercept between the different states and a cost of insertion/removal equal to half the cost of insertion. The distances per phase were normalized (on the largest distance). On the dissimilarity matrix that is produced through this process, we applied a flexible-UPGMA clustering algorithm (Belbin et al., 1992). Eleven clusters were eventually retained, as this is the division that produces the groups that are the most logical and provides robust criteria in response to different tests.

12. More details about the methodology can be found at: https://ollion.cnrs.fr/the-candidates/.
13. Group 7 constitutes a cluster of individuals whose internal consistency is less obvious than the other groups, a frequent outcome in sequence analysis. It is made up of around 20 individuals who had an intermittent involvement in politics and spent a few years in local mandates, or as political assistants before leaving and later returning to elected positions.
14. Interview, March 2019.
15. Interview, July 2017.
16. Quoted in Lefebvre (2019).
17. Issindou (2019, p. 89).
18. Jean-Pierre Raffarin, *France Inter*, April 19, 2017.

Chapter 3

1. These problems are well known to those who use geometric data analysis, and who have long since developed techniques to address them. However, none of the available techniques enables us to address all the problems simultaneously. For more detail, and for a discussion that does justice to these studies, see Boelaert and Ollion (2020).
2. To its practitioners, this may look very similar to what geometric data analysis performs, and at the most general level, it is. But it differs widely in the implementation, and in the output. Instead of transforming the original data into a reduced Euclidean plane, it groups them into cells that are locally connected on a "map." This map is typically a two-dimensional network (reminiscent of a fishing net), in which each cell (a knot in the net) is connected to its immediate neighbors. Each cell corresponds to a so-called prototype in the starting space (a new point in the original data), so that the distance between each observation and each prototype can be computed. The clustering aspect derives directly from these distances: each observation is attributed to the cell whose prototype it is closest to. The optimization (or learning) of a SOM can be thought of as the process of unfolding the net so that it follows the topology of the data as closely as possible. In practice, it consists in iteratively adapting the prototypes: at each iteration, an observation is randomly drawn, its distance toward all prototypes computed, and the closest prototype is chosen. This prototype is then moved closer toward the observation, along with the prototypes of its neighbors on the final map. After a large number of iterations, and if it worked properly, the map represents a discretization of the data which is true to the original topography: cells that are close on the map represent prototypes that are close in the input space, and contain neighboring clusters of original observations. For more details, see (Hastie et al., 2014, chapter 14.4).
3. Field notes, July 25, 2017.
4. Interview with a Socialist MP, 2016.
5. First-time MP (LREM), former local councilor, interviewed in March 2019.
6. First-time MP (LREM), novice, interviewed in March 2019.

NOTES 173

7. First-time MP (LREM), novice, interviewed in March 2019.
8. Field notes, June 20, 2017.
9. Interview, first time MP (LREM), July 2018.
10. Juliette Bresson, *Débuter dans le métier: Le cas des primo-députés du groupe LREM*, mémoire de Master 2, Université de Lille, 2018, pp. 82–83.

Chapter 4

1. Field notes, June 21, 2017.
2. See for instance Lagroye (1994).
3. While it is obviously dependent on place (France) and time (the early 21st century), this analysis tries to go beyond the conventional description of MPs at work, or certain aspects thereof, to expound their lived experience of politics.
4. This analysis is incomplete because it is focused on the aspects of this experience that are considered difficult. It does not emphasize the changes in monetary terms, or in social status that are associated with becoming an MP, which will be discussed in the following chapter.
5. Interview with a first-time MP, former consultant, January 2019.
6. Projet Arcadie, *Rapport sur l'activité réelle des députés*, 2019.
7. Interview, March 2019.
8. Interview, May 2018.
9. Quoted in Cayre (2018, p. 98).
10. Quoted in Cayre (2018, p. 86).
11. Interview, January 2019.
12. Interview with a first time MP (LREM), novice, former consultant, January 2019.
13. Interview with a first-time MP, former primary school teacher.
14. Interview, first-time MP (LREM), January 2019.
15. Political reporter Isabel Hardman offers dozens of similar anecdotes in her recent book, in which she noted that British MPs become, upon election, "fair game for abuse" (Hardman, 2018, p. 44).
16. Interview with a first-time MP (LREM), novice, March 2019.
17. Interview with a political journalist, March 2018.
18. Quoted in Cayre (2018, p. 133).
19. Interview, July 2019.
20. The massive, and most likely unprecedented, wave of staffers who were dismissed six months after the election should be understood in this light. This was an attempt for novice MPs, having realized their mistake, to take control of the situation by employing people who were more knowledgeable about the National Assembly and its functioning. It just happened a little too late for them.
21. Interview with a first-time MP, novice, employee, July 2018.
22. A French TV show detailing the tribes and tribulations of a corrupt politician.
23. Interview, April 2019.
24. Field notes, July 2018.

25. For a detailed description, see Rescan (2019, p. 91).
26. Field notes, July 2018.
27. Interview with a first-time MP, former public servant, political activist for 15 years.
28. Interview with a former parliamentary collaborator, July 9, 2018.

Chapter 5

1. In this respect they are similar to the boxers in the Chicago ghetto studied by Loïc Wacquant. They are the last people to see this activity as a "noble art," where everyone else sees brutality.
2. Interview with an MP *Les Républicains*, March 2015.
3. André Tardieu, *La profession parlementaire*, Flammarion, 1937, p. 31.
4. Session of February 1, 1938.
5. As they are recorded in the *World inequality database,* https://wid.world/
6. Interview, March 2018.
7. Interview, April 2018.
8. For comparative purposes the categories presented in Table 5.1 are those used in French public statistics (the professions and social professional categories nomenclature); they have been translated somewhat freely here so as to be more intuitively understandable for an anglophone audience.
9. Cited in (Delpierre, 2015, pp. 78).
10. See for instance the study by (Cabrera and Webbink, 2019). Although on a different case, it forces us to question the link (long criticized by sociologists of occupation) between diploma, skill, and efficiency in the workplace.

Conclusion

1. This waiting system is sometimes formalized, such as in the tenure track system, where candidates are selected twice, first through the defense of their PhD, and then through recruitment by a university. But even after they have passed these obstacles, they still need to prove their worth—generally by publishing extensively—over a certain period (between four and seven years generally) before being confirmed in their role. If they fail, they find themselves aged around 40 with no job contract and no prospects for employment in the university sector. Imported from the United States, this system is spreading around Europe. After Germany, France has just introduced this kind of position as part of the new law on higher education voted in 2021.
2. It is said that in the USSR under Stalin, the secret service stationed agents in waiting lines to document public opinion. They noted jokes, protests, and personal anecdotes that were exchanged to pass the time and used them as a gauge of what was happening in society. See the book by Sheila Fitzpatrick (2000).

REFERENCES

Abélès, M. (2000). *Un ethnologue à l'Assemblée*. Odile Jacob.

Accominotti, F. (2009). Creativity from interaction: Artistic movements and the creativity careers of modern painters. *Poetics*, 37(3), 267–294.

Achin, C. (2016). Gender and political science: Lessons from the French case. *Italian Political Science*, 11(2), 11–14.

Achin, C., & Lévêque, S. (2007). Femmes, énarques et professionnelles de la politique: Des carrières exceptionnelles sous contraintes. *Genèses*, 67(2), 24–44.

Ackerman, B., & Fishkin, J. S. (2004). *Deliberation Day*. Yale University Press.

Aisenberry, S., & Fasang, A. (2017). The interplay of work and family trajectories over the life course: Germany and the United States in comparison. *American Journal of Sociology*, 122(5), 1448–1484.

Allen, N., Magni, G., Searing, D., & Warncke, P. (2020). What is a career politician? Theories, concepts and measures. *European Political Science Review*, 12(2), 199–217.

Allen, P. (2014). *Bring in the professionals: How pre-parliamentary political experience affects political careers in the House of Commons* [Unpublished doctoral thesis]. Birkbeck, University of London.

Auyero, J. (2012). *Patients of the state: The politics of waiting in Argentina*. Duke University Press.

Bakhtin, M. M. (1981). *The dialogic imagination: Four Essays* (M. Holquist & C. Emerson, Trans.). University of Texas Press.

Barber, S. (2014). Arise, careerless politician: The rise of the professional party leader. *Politics*, 34(1), 23–31.

Bargel, L. (2011). S'attacher à la politique: Carrières de jeunes socialistes professionnels. *Sociétés contemporaines*, 84(4), 79–102.

Behr, V., & Michon, S. (2015). Les cabinets sont-ils une pépinière de futurs ministres? Retour sur les transformations des filières d'accès à la profession politique sous la Cinquième République. In J.-M. Eymeri, X. Bioy, & S. Mouton (Eds.), *Le règne des entourages: Cabinets et conseillers de l'exécutif dans la France contemporaine* (pp. 503–525). Presses de Sciences Po.

Belbin, L., Faith, D. P., & Milligan, G. W. (1992). A comparison of two approaches to beta-flexible clustering. *Multivariate Behavioral Research*, 27(3), 417–433.

Bellon, A., Collas, T., & Mayance, P. (2018). Boulevards et chemins de traverse: Les carrières des collaborateurs de l'exécutif (2012–2014). *Revue française d'administration publique*, 168(4), 875–896.

Best, H., & Cotta, M. (2000). *Parliamentary representatives in Europe, 1848–2000: Legislative recruitment and careers in eleven European countries*. Oxford University Press.

Boelaert, J., Michon, S., & Ollion, É. (2017). *Métier député: Enquête sur la professionnalisation de la politique en France*. Raisons d'agir.

Boelaert, J., & Ollion, É. (2020). Les sommets du Palais: Analyser l'espace parlementaire avec des cartes auto-organisatrices. *Revue française de science politique, 3* (2020), 373–398.

Borchert, J., & Zeiss, J. (Eds.). (2003). *The political class in advanced democracies*. Oxford University Press.

Bovens, M., & Wille, A. (2017). *Diploma democracy: The rise of political meritocracy*. Oxford University Press.

Bresson, J. (2018). *Débuter dans le métier: Le cas des primo-députés du groupe LREM* [Unpublished master's thesis]. Lille University.

Bresson, J., & Ollion, É. (2022). Que sont les députés novices devenus. Sociologie d'une promesse non tenue. In Bernard Dolez, Julien Fretel, & Rémi Lefebvre (Eds.), *L'entreprise Macron à l'épreuve du pouvoir*. Presses universitaires de Grenoble.

Buge, É., & Ollion, É. (2022). Que vaut un député? Ce que l'indemnité dit du mandat (1914–2020). *Annales: Histoire, sciences sociales, 78*(3), 703–737.

Cabrera, J. M., & Webbink, D. (2019). Do higher salaries yield better teachers and better student outcomes? *Journal of Human Resources, 55*(4), 1222–1257.

Cagé, J. (2020). *The price of democracy: How money shapes politics and what to do about it*. Harvard University Press.

Cairney, P. (2007). The professionalisation of MPs: Refining the "politics-facilitating" explanation. *Parliamentary Affairs, 60*(2), 212–233.

Campbell, R., Childs, S., & Lovenduski, J. (2010). Do women need women representatives? *British Journal of Political Science, 40*(1), 171–194.

Canon, D. T. (1990). *Actors, athletes, and astronauts: Political amateurs in the United States congress*. University of Chicago Press.

Canon, D. T. (2011). The year of the outsider: Political amateurs in the U.S. congress. *The Forum, 8*(4), 1–14.

Carnes, N. (2012). Does the numerical underrepresentation of the working class in congress matter? *Legislative Studies Quarterly, 37*(1), 5–34.

Carnes, N. (2020). *The cash ceiling: Why only the rich run for office—and what we can do about it*. Princeton University Press.

Cayre, E. (2018). *Itinéraire d'un élu novice à l'Assemblée nationale: La fabrique du député au cœur du travail parlementaire* [Unpublished master's thesis]. EHESS.

Coenen-Huther, J. (1992). Production informelle des normes: Les files d'attente en Russie soviétique. *Revue française de sociologie, 33*(2), 213–232.

Collas, T. (2018). Multiphase sequence analysis. In G. Ritschard & M. Studer (Eds.), *Sequence analysis and related approaches: Innovative methods and applications* (pp. 149–166). Springer International.

Collovald, A. (1989). Les poujadistes, ou l'échec en politique. *Revue d'Histoire Moderne & Contemporaine, 36*(1), 113–133.

Cos, R. (2019). De la dénégation du programme à la baisse de la fiscalité du capital. In B. Dolez, J. Fretel, & R. Lefebvre (Eds.), *L'entreprise Macron* (pp. 39–51). Presses universitaires de Grenoble.

Costa, O., & Poyet, C. (2016). Back to their roots: French MPs in their district. *French Politics, 14*(4), 406–438.

Cowley, P. (2012). Arise, novice leader! The continuing rise of the career politician in Britain. *Politics, 32*(1), 31–38.

Crewe, E. (2015). *The House of Commons: An anthropology of MPs at work*. Bloomsbury Academic.

Damamme, D. (1999). Professionnel de la politique, un métier peu avouable. In M. Offerlé (Ed.), *La profession politique: XIXe–XXe siècles* (pp. 37–67). Belin.

DeGregorio, C. (1995). Staff utilization in the U.S. Congress: Committee chairs and senior aides. *Polity, 28*(2), 261–275.

Delpierre, A. (2015). *"Une fois l'émission faite, j'ai senti qu'on me regardait à l'Assemblée": Rapports à la médiatisation et pratiques de communication des élus; Une enquête auprès des députés français* [Unpublished master's thesis]. École normale supérieure and EHESS.

Demazière, D., & Le Lidec, P. (Eds.). (2014). *Les mondes du travail politique: Les élus et leurs entourages*. Presses universitaires de Rennes.

Dogan, M. (1967). Les filières de la carrière politique en France. *Revue française de sociologie, 8*(4), 468–492.

Denord, F., & Lagneau-Ymonet, P. (2016). *Le concert des puissants*. Raisons d'agir.

Evans, G., & Tilley, J. (2017). *The new politics of class: The political exclusion of the British working class*. Oxford University Press.

Fenno, R. F. (2003). *Home style: House members in their districts*. Longman.

Fertikh, K. (2020). *L'invention de la social-démocratie allemande: Une histoire sociale du programme Bad Godesberg*. Éditions de la Maison des sciences de l'homme.

Fitzpatrick, S. (Ed.). (2000). *Stalinism: New Directions*. Routledge.

François, A., & Grossman, E. (2011). Who are the deputies of the Fifth Republic? Some figures. *French Politics, 9*(4), 364–380.

François, B. (2011). *Le régime politique de la Ve République*. La Découverte.

Gaïti, B. (1999). Les incertitudes des origines: Mai 58 et la Ve République. *Politix: Revue des sciences sociales du politique, 12*(47), 27–62.

Gaxie, D. (2000). *La démocratie représentative* (3rd ed.). Montchrestien.

Ginzburg, L. (1995). *The Blockade Diary*. Penguin.

Goffman, E. (1967). *Interaction ritual: Essays on face-to-face behavior*. Doubleday.

Hagevi, M. (2003). Sweden: Between participation ideal and professionalism. In J. Borchert and J. Zeiss (Eds.), *The political class in advanced democracies: A comparative handbook* (pp. 352–373). Oxford University Press.

Halpin, B., & Chan, T. W. (1998). Class careers as sequences: An optimal matching analysis of work-life histories. *European Sociological Review, 14*(2), 111–130.

Hardman, I. (2018). *Why we get the wrong politicians: Shortlisted for the Waterstones Book of the Year*. Atlantic Books.

Hassin, R., & Haviv, M. (2003). *To queue or not to queue: Equilibrium behavior in queueing systems*. Kluwer Academic.

Hastie, T. et al. (2009). *The elements of statistical learning: Data mining, inference, and prediction*. Springer.

Hix, S., & Noury, A. (2007). Politics, not economic interests: Determinants of migration policies in the European Union. *International Migration Review, 41*(1), 182–205.

Ismard, P. (2015). *La Démocratie contre les experts: Les esclaves publics en Grèce ancienne*. Seuil.

Issindou, M. (2019). *Tourments au Palais Bourbon: Chroniques d'un député socialiste*. Presses universitaires de Grenoble.

Jahoda, M., Lazarsfeld, P. F., & Zeisel, H. (2017 [1933]). *Marienthal: The sociography of an unemployed community*. Routledge.

Kavanagh, D. (1995). *Election campaigning: The new marketing of politics*. Blackwell.

King, A. (1981). The rise of the career politician in Britain—and its consequences. *British Journal of Political Science*, *11*(3), 249–285.

Kohonen, T. (1997). Exploration of very large databases by self-organizing maps. Proceedings of international conference on neural networks. Vol. 1. IEEE.

Kousser, T. (2005). *Term limits and the dismantling of state legislative professionalism*. Cambridge University Press.

Lagroye, J. (1994). Être du métier. *Politix: Revue des sciences sociales du politique*, *7*(28), 5–15.

Laurison, D. (2022). *Producing politics: Inside the exclusive campaign world where the privileged few shape politics for all of us*. Beacon Press.

Lebaron, F., & Le Roux, B. (2013). Géométrie du champ. *Actes de la recherche en sciences sociales*, *5*, 106–109.

Lefebvre, R. (2014). Les élus comme entrepreneurs de temps: Les agendas des cumulants. In D. Demazière & P. Le Lidec (Eds.), *Les mondes du travail politique: Les élus et leurs entourages* (pp. 53–70). Presses universitaires de Rennes.

Lefebvre, R. (2019). Les députés en marche! Issus du parti socialiste: Sociologie d'une migration partisane. In B. Dolez, J. Fretel, & R. Lefebvre (Eds.), *L'entreprise Macron* (pp. 229–242). Presses universitaires de Grenoble.

Lefebvre, R., & Sawicki, F. (2006). *La société des socialistes: Le PS aujourd'hui*. Croquant.

Lesnard, L. (2008). Off-scheduling within dual-earner couples: An unequal and negative externality for family time. *American Journal of Sociology*, *114*(2), 447–490.

Mahler, M. (2011). The day before election day. *Ethnography*, *12*(2), 149–173.

Mansbridge, J. (1999). Should blacks represent blacks and women represent women? A contingent "yes." *Journal of Politics*, *61*(3), 628–657.

Martigny, V. (2017). À gauche, la fin de la synthèse social-démocrate. In P. Perrineau (Ed.), *Le vote disruptif: Les élections présidentielle et législatives de 2017* (pp. 43–58). Presses de Sciences Po.

Matthews, D. R. (1960). *U.S. senators and their world*. University of North Carolina Press.

Matthews, D. R. (1984). Legislative recruitment and legislative careers. *Legislative Studies Quarterly*, *9*(4), 547–585.

Michon, S. (2014). Composition et organisation de l'entourage des eurodéputés français: Spécificités et logiques de structuration des équipes parlementaires. In D. Demazière & P. Le Lidec (Eds.), *Les mondes du travail politique: Les élus et leurs entourages* (pp. 125–141). Presses universitaires de Rennes.

Michon, S. (2019). L'entreprise chevillée au corps: L'entrée d'une "société civile" entrepreneuriale à l'Assemblée. In B. Dolez, J. Fretel, & R. Lefebvre (Eds.), *L'entreprise Macron* (pp. 217–228). Presses universitaires de Grenoble.

Michon, S., & Ollion, É. (2018). Retour sur la professionnalisation politique: Revue de littérature critique et perspectives. *Sociologie du travail*, *60*(1). https://doi.org/10.4000/sdt.1706.

Mudde, C., & Kaltwasser, C. R. (2013). Exclusionary vs. inclusionary populism: Comparing contemporary Europe and Latin America. *Government and Opposition*, *48*(2), 147–174.

Norris, P., & Lovenduski, J. (1995). *Political recruitment: Gender, race and class in the British Parliament*. Cambridge University Press.

Offerlé, M. (1984). Illégitimité et légitimation du personnel politique ouvrier en France avant 1914. *Annales*, *39*(4), 681–716.

Offerlé, M. (2019). "Les patrons" ou "des patrons" avec Emmanuel Macron: Capitaux entrepreneuriaux et capital politique. In B. Dolez, J. Fretel, & R. Lefebvre (Eds.), *L'entreprise Macron* (pp. 79–92). Presses universitaires de Grenoble.

Ohmura, T., Bailer, S., Meiβner, P., & Selb, P. (2018). Party animals, career changers and other pathways into parliament. *West European Politics, 41*(1), 169–195.

Phélippeau, É. (2002). *L'invention de l'homme politique moderne: Mackau, l'Orne et la République.* Belin.

Phillips, A. (1995). *The politics of presence.* Clarendon Press.

Pitkin, H. F. (1967). *The concept of representation.* University of California Press.

Price, H. D. (1975). Congress and the evolution of legislative professionalism. In N. J. Ornstein (Ed.), *Congress in change: Evolution and reform* (p. 2–23). Praeger.

Pudal, B. (1989). *Prendre parti: Pour une sociologie historique du PCF.* Presses de la Fondation nationale des sciences politiques.

Rescan, M. (2019). *Les Grandes illusions: Enquête sur les soldats de la macronie.* Robert Laffont.

Reskin, B., & Roos, P. (1990). *Job queues, gender queues: Explaining women's inroads into male occupations.* Temple University Press.

Rice, S. A. (1927). The identification of blocs in small political bodies. *American Political Science Review, 21*(3), 619–627.

Riddell, P. (1995). The impact of the rise of the career politician. *Journal of Legislative Studies, 1*(2), 186–191.

Rosa, H. (2013). *Social acceleration: A new theory of modernity.* Columbia University Press. (Original work published 2005)

Sansu, M. (2022). *PolitTweets. La communication politique des députés.* Master's Thesis in Sociology. ENS Paris-Saclay.

Sartre, J.-P. (1976). *Critique of dialectical reason* (J. Ree, Ed.; A. Sheridan-Smith, Trans.; Vol. 1). New Left Books. (Original work published 1960)

Sawicki, F. (1994). Laurent Fabius: Du "Giscard de gauche" au "socialiste moderne." *Pôle Sud, 1*(1), 35–60.

Sawicki, F. (1999). Classer les hommes politiques: Les usages des indicateurs de position sociale pour la compréhension de la professionnalisation politique. In M. Offerlé (Ed.), *La profession politique: XIXe–XXe siècles* (pp. 135–170). Belin.

Schlackman, R., & Douglas, J. (1995). Attack mail: The silent killer. *Campaigns and Elections, 25–26,* 16–17.

Schwartz, B. (1974). Waiting, exchange, and power: The distribution of time in social systems. *American Journal of Sociology, 79*(4), 841–870.

Searing, D. (1994). *Westminster's world: Understanding political roles.* Harvard University Press.

Strudel, S. (2017). Emmanuel Macron: Un oxymore politique? In P. Perrineau (Ed.), *Le vote disruptif* (pp. 205–220). Presses de Sciences Po.

Turner-Zwinkels, T., & Mills, M. C. (2020). Pathways to power: The role of preparliamentary careers and political human capital in the obtainment of cabinet positions. *Legislative Studies Quarterly, 45*(2), 207–252.

Villani, C. (2019). *Immersion: De la science au Parlement.* Flammarion.

Wacquant, L. (2011). Habitus as topic and tool: Reflections on becoming a prizefighter. *Qualitative Research in Psychology, 8*(1), 81–92.

Wacquant, L. (2015). For a sociology of flesh and blood. *Qualitative Sociology, 38*(1), 1–11.

Weber, M. (1946). Politics as a vocation: Lecture to the free students society at Munich university, January 1919. In C. Wright Mills & H. H. Gerth (Eds.), *From Max Weber: Essays in sociology* (pp. 77–128). Oxford University Press. (Original work published 1919)

Wilson, J. Q. (1962). *The amateur Democrat: Club politics in three cities*. University of Chicago Press.

Yong, B., & Hazell, R. (2014). *Special advisers: Who they are, what they do and why they matter*. Hart.

INDEX

For the benefit of digital users, indexed terms that span two pages (e.g., 52–53) may, on occasion, appear on only one of those pages.

Allen, Peter, 6–7, 8–9
amateurs. *See* novice MPs
Auyero, Javier, 19–20, 102

Bourdieu, Pierre, 34–35, 47, 74, 85–86, 121, 144

Capra, Frank, 79, 106
career politicians
    change in careers, 29–36
    compensation of (*see* political condition)
    criticism of, 3–4, 24, 25–26, 28–29, 39–40
    cursus honorum, 32
    definition, 61–62
    living for politics, 27–28
    living off politics, 27–28
    and populism, 39–43
computational social sciences
    and ethnography, 11
    machine learning, 86–92

digital data
    problems with, 55, 83–84
    use of, 81, 84–85

École nationale d'administration (ENA), 24–25, 50–51, 139, 142–43
electoral campaigns, 2–3, 23, 39–40, 43–47, 58
En Marche!. *See* La République en Marche

French Communist Party (PCF), 34, 58, 138–39
French Revolution, 5, 132–33

Front National (FN). *See* Rassemblement national

Goffman, Erving, 119, 120–21

Italy, 4, 40

King, Anthony, 61–62

La France Insoumise (LFI), 37, 40–41, 92
La République en Marche (LREM), 1–2, 24–25, 40–41, 52–53, 58, 60–61, 81, 92, 95–96, 122, 124
    campaign, 69–70, 73–74
    and populism, 39–43

Macron, Emmanuel
    anti-professional rhetoric, 24–25
    campaign promises, 7, 14–15, 52
    career, 1–4, 7, 9, 10, 13, 17
    electoral campaign, 7, 17, 43–47, 77–78
    lack of experience, 75–77, 155
Mudde, Cas, 41, 42–43

novice MPs, 21–22, 52–54, 79–81
    as analyzers of politics, 109–13
    causes of relegation, 96–101, 164–65
    civil society, 52–53
    influence in parliament, 82–85

parliament
    discovery of, 1–2
    as hierarchical differentiated spaces, 85–96
    history, 132–33
    organization, 54
    social composition of (*see* representative democracy)

political condition
  and anonymity, 116–21
  and compensation, 132–37
  and *Homo politicus*, 14, 17–21
  and journalism, 123–24, 164
  and relationship to time, 109–13
  texture of, 108–9
  and violence, 121–29
  and work, 132–37
political experience
  and *illusio*, 121, 143–51
  and political practice, 6–9, 92–96
  and political success, 5–9, 92–96
  varieties of, 62–68
professional politicians. *See* career politicians

Rassemblement National (RN). 31–32
representative democracy
  and direct democracy, 4–5
  and experience (*see* political experience)
  and gender parity, 55–56, 59, 75, 105
  and social representativity, 56, 60–61, 138–39
  and sortition by lot, 4–5
  substantive representation, 5–6

Sartre, Jean-Paul, 156
Mr. Smith goes to Washington (1939), 79, 106
Socialist Party (PS), 2, 43–44, 45–46, 141–42
Spain, 4
Sweden, 29

United States of America, 4, 40

Wacquant, Loïc, 108, 115
wait. *See* waiting lines
waiting line
  and collective action
  cutting in the, 53–54, 73–74
  effects of, 96–106, 154–56
  moral economy of the, 74–78
  political professionalization as, 17–18
  in politics, 17–21, 36
  and social recruitment, 141–43
  theory of, 154–59
  in the USSR, 75
Weber, Max, 17–18, 26–28, 50–51